FIGHTING THE DEVE

Gerald Moore graduated from Guy's Hospital. He holds post graduate degrees in medicine and dentistry. He is the author of several highly successful books including a widely acclaimed autobiography *Treading in Treacle* and five volumes of poetry. He gave up his Harley Street practice in 1986 and now lives in North Devon, a region of outstanding natural beauty whose protection has now become his abiding passion. His home environment is the scene of the events described in this book. He was responsible for organising the protest group whose campaign against the developers was so successful.

Adrian Moore is the son of Gerald Moore. He is Parish and District Councillor for Whealden, East Sussex and sits on the planning committees of both. In this capacity he has assisted in the formation of the District Plan which acts as the basis for planning and development policy for the district. He is much reported and quoted in area planning politics and has written extensively on these interests in regional publications.

To Ruth, Charlotte and Janet.

FIGHTING
THE
DEVELOPERS

GERALD MOORE AND ADRIAN MOORE

First published in 1991
by
Patton Publications
Orchard House
Swimbridge
Barnstaple
North Devon
EX32 OPL

Distributed
by
Ruskin Book Services
Marlborough House
Marlborough Street
Kidderminster
Worcestershire
DY10 1BJ

BRITISH LIBRARY CATALOGUING IN PUBLICATION DATA

Fighting the developers: planning protest.
1. Environment. Planning. Public participation of
711.12

Set in 10 on 12 Times Roman
Copy preparation by Patton Publications
Printed and bound in Great Britain
by
BPCC Wheatons Ltd, Exeter

ISBN 1 872426 02 6 Hardback

ISBN 1 872426 03 4 Paperback

CONTENTS

AUTHORS' NOTE

The campaign discussed in this book took place in a village and we have referred throughout to District and Parish Councils who administer local government in rural areas. In London and other urban areas, councils have other titles appropriate to the districts they serve and the reader should be alert to this detail.

The real life events described in this book are related in order to give the reader first hand knowledge of how to fight developers, not to identify individuals or comment on their role.

1

THE REASON WHY

This book aims to give practical advice to whoever seeks guidance on ways of organising effective opposition to developers whose schemes are seen to be undesirable or damaging to home environments or community locations.

The authors use the text from time to time to consider wider environmental issues, for whenever a tree is felled or grass buried under tarmac, another little desert is created. Reasons will always be given, argued and justified to substantiate a logic for 'need and progress'. We all see these small deserts are growing. We know they are dead earth and where they exist, so dies our present delight and the fertile future of our children. It is the authors' conviction that the planet's life-sustaining capability will be saved by individuals who are prepared to find time to fight off threats to the natural world, even if their threatened bit of nature merely comprises a patch of grass or flowering tree at the end of their street.

As the narrative is developed and where appropriate to the case, opportunity is taken to address the many conflicting moral considerations that inevitably arise. To begin with, since the authors applaud the basic human urges underlying today's home owning society, there appears to be no good reason for dithering over adopting a group identity. Fortunately, the recently coined term 'Nimby' (N.ot I.n M.y B.ack Y.ard) is conveniently to hand. Origins and a wider definition are given later. For the moment we can say that Nimbys have probably been around since the Stone Age. However, today's Nimby cult is a phenomenon of Britain's property-owning society. It is rooted in the desire for stability and security every right minded human-being is entitled to enjoy within the home and its surroundings. No political affiliation is claimed, nor is the cult tagged to any ideologies.

If you have a roof over your head, whether from ownership or any other right of tenure and if you have browsed this far, buy the book and read on.

Our home environment means all things to all people. Once we have settled in, we begin to develop sharpened attitudes towards changes within that location and resent anything seen as a threat to the existing state of things. Since life does not deal in certainties, all home environments are vulnerable and at risk. In the real world, thrusting, powerful and often self-interested human-beings are restlessly examining the unsuspecting individual's place of habitation with a view to changing it to fulfill their own notion of progress or gain!

Until recent times, few citizens happily pursuing their own lives, would have denied such enterprise freedoms. Modern Britain owes its evolution to such striving. Concepts of live- and-let-live fit comfortably into our historic democratic perspectives. Furthermore, we are not arguing that this is a bad thing. Urban renewal is rarely regarded with apprehension by most people. However, within much of todays planning framework, society is increasingly encountering developments that are bad and need to be contested. The complex threats to earth's survival offers this stark conclusion: all activity, however localised, indisputably seen to be environmentally destructive, must be stopped when and wherever possible – even though the organisations involved claim to be fulfilling human needs. This recognition has created the NIMBY.

We claim nothing more for this concise book beyond giving a practical description of embryo NIMBYS' campaigning in a rural backwater. Our conflict with planners and developers involved us for the first time in our lives with issues so profound in their wider implications, we can never again take for granted any of the irreplaceable living treasures that flourish at our feet. From now on we can never stand by and allow the bulldozers to crush these treasures out of existence.

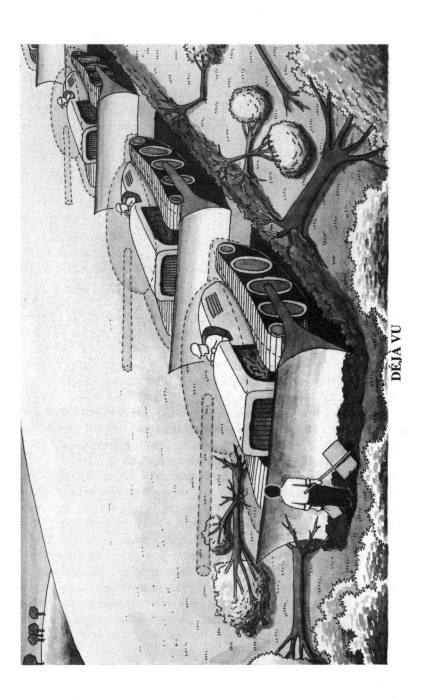

DÉJÀ VU

The planet is overcrowded. No-one denies this. In cities and urban areas we are surrounded with hard evidence that man has reached crisis point. This is a small island and we draw no comfort from the fact that the greatest population explosions are taking place in under-developed countries. There has been a dramatic growth in Britain's indigenous population since World War II. Small wonder that increasing numbers of us crave for islands of social peace, offering respite from the hectic pressures of daily life! As recently as thirty years ago, those of us who lived through that period would have questioned such assertion as overstating the case. This, in our view, identifies the growing scale of urban man's predicament.

The 'rat syndrome' is now valid in medical thinking. Much of what is grouped under the term 'stress' represents a vast progression of unhealthy social evolution. Medical waiting rooms are packed with its victims! How do we remain sane in an increasingly intrusive world? Undoubtedly people do need people and we are not suggesting that the remedy lies in a monastery. No man is an island. But green space is vanishing and current legislation, stretching to meet social demands, is geared up to accelerate this loss. As the situation worsens increasing numbers of normally passive citizens find themselves, either in groups or as individuals, arming to fight planning bureaucracy hellbent on pushing through schemes that people neither respect the need for nor want.

This proposition will, of course, be seen by many to be riddled with contradictions and anomalies. Human interests are hotbeds of conflict. One man's legitimate aspirations are another man's living hell!

Deprived families in our burgeoning population cry out to be decently housed and gainfully employed. Yet this manifestly moral right is poised to bury under concrete every green acre in sight. More distantly, it is felling forests and turning untold fertile acres into deserts. Where do these remote populations go when their lands no longer support them ? Who feeds them when our own land barely feeds us ? Democracy and freedom have always been strapped to a powder keg with a lit fuse. Those of us who believe that the human race faces planetary catastrophe see recent events dramatically shortening the fuse. The worst scientific scenario predicts the end of the world, as we know it today, within the lifetime of children now being born.

We do not pretend to offer solutions in these pages.

Consider below a wise man offering us the first contradiction:

'It has been truly said that the best government is no government.'

The American reformer and philosopher Wendell Phillips put the fact another way when he said:

'All governing over-much kills the self-help and energy of the governed.'

How well this concept suits our dream of liberty for the whole of mankind. Yet few societies are adult enough and certainly not far-sighted enough to put life-values before self. We do know, however, that problems bigger than individuals and nations are taking hold of human destiny. The planet is sick and possibly dying. Man knows the cure: pure air, sweet water, lush meadows and living oceans and forests. Presently we are prescribing and dispensing poisons. Every sane person knows this must stop. This NIMBY GUIDE to the defence of everymans' treasured plot begins with a valley, a green valley, rich, idyllic and half as old as time.

2

THE NIMBY – FLESH AND BLOOD

Despite what was said earlier to justify the adoption of the term Nimby, readers may still have lingering doubts about aligning themselves with social groupings that can be dismissed in derogatory terms, connected in certain undefined ways with antisocial attitudes that work against the common weal. We have in mind the move towards denigrating the Yuppy despite the fact that many people are pleased to identify themselves as such, since they recognise their usefulness as productive members of the nation's workforce and seek to gain private advantage as such.

One is hard pressed to condense into a single and explicit term a growing national philosophy that seeks to embrace so many critical and urgent concerns. However one may feel that the term Nimby lacks the sympathetic colour of say an evangelist, its origin as a term of abuse in circumstances that most thinking people will applaud, convinces us that no better name can be given to all those citizens who see the assault on the environment in which they live and beyond as unacceptable.

THE NIMBY DEFINED

A leading national newspaper included, in the middle of a larger article on a planning dispute, the following apocalyptic quote:

'Housing needs should over-ride local objectors. In this context, objectors who place their own narrow interests before this need are NIMBYS.'

Nicholas Ridley, former Minister of the Environment.

Ridley gave us a name, identity and purpose. It may be his only footnote in history. Since it is likely that the term will become established in the English language, we restate it formally in what we hope will become the model for all dictionary definitions:

NIMBY *n.* [NEW ENG.] An acronym of N.ot I.n M.y B.ack Y.ard. Originally it was coined derisively, but it is now seen as denoting individuals or groups waging David and Goliath battles to save treasured corners of their environment from the predatory intentions of powerful vested interests or selfish private individuals.

The man who said that 'An Englishman's home is his castle', defined the true Nimby. He could have added that beyond the Englishmans' castle wall stretches his garden fiefdom and beyond this hallowed enclosure, his parish kingdom.

It is reassuring to recognise that this concept of the British as Nimbys has an honourable precedent in the nation's social history. From earliest times it has shaped the fundamental social order of our state and identified the prime communal role of the individual, be he prince or commoner.

No other nation in Europe places so much emphasis on home ownership as the British. Few Britons would deny sharing the dream of having 'a place of their own' and put the greater part of their working life's effort into achieving the ambition.

From our original definition, the Nimby is the basic unit of our property-owning democracy. Even before the term was coined, Nimby culture was long regarded as a major cohesive force of the nation. The desirability of making this feature of our society universal is a fact of social logic and equity. Besides, it is a social ideal that translates easily into the realities of peoples' political beliefs. Property-owners are to all intent and purpose in control of their own lives – a unit of self government within the corporate body of the state. There is enough substance in all this to argue for the 'acceptable face of Nimbyism'. When it is condemned, one is listening to the sillier wranglings of those who pander to easy anti-elitist prejudices. Societies need to recognise and respect the sources of their strength. Property ownership is a core factor in maintaining what is singularly the best of the British way of life. Newcomers to our country readily adapt to its values, recognising its virtues with the same enthusiasm as native born British.

UNITED NIMBYS BECOME A VOICE OF CONSCIENCE

As well as opposing environmental destruction in the wider context, Nimbys can exert a controlling influence on the decisions of planners and developers. Furthermore, they can adjudicate on what these individuals and groups try to put into the landscape. They can demand that those with the power to affect the destiny of the areas in which we live, reinstate in their portfolio of civic values: beauty, harmony, elegance and tranquility. Until everyone recognises our living environment's health depends on these elements – and the contribution they make to 'urban sanity', we will never ensure that the public mind rejects easy tolerance of urban neglect, filth, decay and dereliction. Furthermore until these issues are firmly addressed, it hardly needs to be emphasised that this island could soon cease to be a fit place in which to live.

Mankind faces a gathering prospect of ecological destruction. Its grave implications include doubts as to the chances of human survival. Ways of solving the problem largely rests with people who cherish their own living space. Such people are far more likely to reflect on their material good fortune, yet ponder their abundance in a wiser frame of mind. They are the people who must link increasing social tolerance amid prosperity to an intolerance of waste, neglect and urban abuse. We live in a world vulnerable to human error – we are obliged to accept this – but man-made disasters require much organisation; a chain reaction linking multiple errors of judgement, ignorance, greed and lack of vision. The list could be made endless.

Acknowledging this truth opens our minds to ways and means. It then becomes possible to mount intelligent survival campaigns. Individuals must stop feeling helpless in the midst of the welter of events and decision making to which they have no access – to which they feel marginal and so it seems, have no influencing voice. We can all recognise the factors that disfigure our streets or our regions. If we maintain that there is little we can do about these problems, we will continue to trivialise them and put up with them.

THE MAN WHO SOLD HIS BACK YARD

What do we really mean by progress and necessity? How many of us recognise the great social and commercial pressures breaching the checks and loosening the brakes on planning, built into those words? How often, in consequence, do the relaxed responses of planning authorities display no thought to their decision making ?

It is clear that corporate bodies nationwide are making a science of stratagems designed to get around planning rules and obstacles, whatever form they take. The financial stakes are now so high in many environmentally damaging development proposals, that big business affords to meet the disproportionate costs required to find loopholes in planning laws. The best legal and planning brains are paid highly to find ways of loosening or circumventing obstructive planning regulations. Those in opposition will rarely have resources on such a scale to meet these forces head-on – only guile and skill coupled with intelligent research will prevail!

Every year 75,000 acres of rural land is lost forever to developers. In the main we are blind to this. In ten years from now, if present trends continue, a currently unspoilt region of Britain, in area the size of the county of Bedfordshire, will be buried under tarmac and concrete. Trees, grass, lakes and rivers, not to mention fine old architecture and other artifacts that identify local history, give districts their character and culture, will vanish.

If this trend translates into the next century, it is unlikely that our society will survive the consequences. We must also take account of the fact that today's regional destruction mirrors what is happening in the rest of the world. In looking at what goes on in our domestic environment, Britain can no longer regard itself as an island; when the bell tolls, it will be tolling for the planet.

BALANCING SOCIAL REPONSIBILITY

From Land's End to John O'Groats, urban man has reached a bleak juncture. Presently there is within reachable distance open unspoilt countryside. This still commonplace amenity is increasingly threatened by today's land-hungry planning policies. It could be argued that we have only ourselves to blame. Here again needs and contradictions confuse the thrust of logic. Homelessness is increasing. We live with a permanent housing crisis that demands to be resolved! The moral imperative to get on with the job is overwhelming and an impatient attitude is no bad thing, when confronting what has correctly been described as the delays and insolence of office. Bureaucracy is a crushing institution when it is not working efficiently in the interests of every section of our society, especially the dispossessed. But urban growth and remodelling is an organic matter and must evolve organically. It is multi-dimensional and multi-factorial. We rush all change at the peril of the environment and at risk to ourselves. Such is the scale and complexity of the social dilemma.

Too many people also refuse to reject the old maxim that 'where there's muck, there's brass'. The only context in which this remains true is when we recycle the muck we create. Human muck (and this includes bad urban development as well as discarded cola cans and burger wrappers) fouling up the environment in which we live is the greatest index of human social failure and the greatest outward sign of human social illiteracy. We either learn to regard its unchallenged presence in our streets and landscapes as an insult to human dignity and hygiene, or we will be forced to wallow in it as the ultimate instrument — apart from atomic war — of human extinction.

Reclaim — Recycle — Renovate — Renew — must become the four 'Rs' of the age in which we live.

'Keep Nature's great original in view.'

P Francis. — Horace, Art of Poetry.

Yet there need be no conflict of interest as far as land use is concerned. A visionary approach to city land reclamation and urban renewal would solve, at a stroke, most of the destructive activity currently devastating our historic cities and rural heartland. Furthermore it is in the cities where the largest number of people want to live.

Few of us are naturally able to articulate our spiritual needs. Even fewer appear to correctly value the contribution made by the untramelled elements of the natural world to the balance of the human mind. If we lose rural Britain, we lose one of the great panaceas available to the human spirit. The bliss one experiences in an unspoilt landscape is intangible but vital — a basic necessity of life that sustains our health like love, food and sleep. It renews our minds by reflecting the timeless order of planet earth.

La verdad ses sempre verde — *Truth is always green.*

Old Spanish proverb.

3

THE VALLEY VILLAGE

The locations named in the text have been deliberately changed to avoid the slight possibility of offence or embarrassment to anyone who might choose to link their place of residence or personal interests to the narrative.

This book records the real-life experience of a group of villagers who, at the outset of the events related, were hardly known to each other. Strangers who came together in common cause to fight a planning application to build a housing estate in an unspoilt valley, whose proximity to the heart of the village gave the parish environment its unique rural character.

Many old residents, especially those born and bred in the vicinity, perhaps over-familiar with its charm, seemed indifferent, even contemptuous of the natural paradise good fortune and place of birth had bequeathed them. They refused to join the action. But what was at risk rallied the perceptive and determined lovers of vanishing rural Britain. The action taken to create a wider local awareness and organise the business of protest and carry it through to a successful conclusion, proved rich in 'experience lived through and lessons drawn'.

This account describes how we stumbled through the opening phase of our campaign. It goes on to present the method and techniques we learnt and employed for co-ordinating our protest. We were lucky, the whole exercise cost little beyond time and petty cash.

We were favoured with adverse environmental factors working against the developers. It cannot be claimed that all local planning disputes will be resolved with such ease. The strategy we employed has enough common factors to cover most cases likely to be encountered and optimism must stand beside enthusiasm in life if anything is to come of personal endeavours.

DEVELOPMENT FEARS CONFIRMED
WE CONFRONT THE UNKNOWN

Planning politics today are minefields. The straightforward surface appearance of things disguises a warren of intrigue and insider dealing. This is not intended to accuse men in public office of corrupt practices, but to remind readers of the uncomfortable fact that IN-SIDERS know each other, share friendships, have common interests and common sentiments. The public on the outside of politics encourages this by rarely being interested in what is going on about them, until emergent consequences begin to hurt.

Men and women of public office, long practiced in bureaucratic craft, frequently arrogate to themselves impregnable certainties; they KNOW what is good for the people they are elected to serve! Armed with their certainties they stride forward, invincibly convinced of their personal and corporate rectitude. The authors are reluctant to squeeze great moments of history into the readers' concerns, but it is worth a moment's pause to add that politics are full of the maligned consequences of such thinking. Rousseau, the notable eighteenth century philosopher, whose views helped shape the political attitudes of his day was credited with saying:

'A nation's leaders know what is good for the great majority of the people much better than the great majority know what is good for itself.'

We have isolated the thought to make a point:

In a period of bad government, new leadership made this sound attractive to a largely ignorant peasantry. Undoubtedly the new political forces believed what they preached, but it proved to be an insider prescription for the old power game. With the advent of the

Revolution, the thought was put to the test. Led by a self-proclaimed democratic leadership, France undoubtedly thought it a sound doctrine as it watched a corrupt and doomed aristocracy perish under the guillotine. When it led inevitably to the reign of terror and a largely innocent section of the population shared the same fate, the silent majority turned on their erstwhile leaders and repaid the years of killing with the same instrument. We all know there are even more appalling examples in recent world history that have created even greater degrees of human misery through failures of political judgement.

Yet despite these historic lessons, who would deny that this thinking is just as prevalent and influential today.

Reflection:

'Government is a trust and the officers of the government are trustees; and both the trust and the trustees are created for the benefit of the people.'

H Clay. American Statesman. (d. 1852).

4

GENESIS OF CONFLICT

'Life everywhere will swallow a man, unless he rise vigorously and try to swallow it.'

Thomas Carlyle. Great English Writer. (d.1881)

Patfield Moor is an ancient village clustering a twelfth century church and nestling in the valley folds of a unique complex of rounded hills. They could be properly described as anatomical, fertile and feminine; all of which hardly needs us to stress that they are beautiful!

To the east of the village, untrespassed for the past thousand years, lies a level valley bounded by the same lovely hills and traversed by a placid, meandering river. The river is home to heron, kingfishers and ducks; it is richly framed by trees and abounds with fish. The valley is designated a region of outstanding landscape value.

In winter the valley plain is prone to flood. In an area where flat land is at a premium it presents to the minds of speculators an ideal zone for village expansion.

PRISONERS OF HISTORY

Before taking the reader into the practical realms of the protest we pause to add an introspective study of the village soul.

Village mentality is special; the shape of the dispute turned principally on the quirks, character and contradictions of village thinking.

This we now observe in the study given below.

Village communities are all about themselves and their past. They live their present by recycling their histories. They are all about continuity and a love-hate for discontinuity; conditioned by tradition and reluctant outlook. This set traps of their own making. Collective thinking based on age-old prejudices frequently puts unjustified obstacles in the way of clarifying 'public interest', noticeably when faced with opposing demands of development and conservation.

A good example is provided by the lack of judgement displayed when distinguishing real needs from those that are simply imagined or invented. Timeless beliefs and folklore philosophies also help create opaque mentalities, often turning idiosyncratic thinking into formidable barriers to rational decisions; their public bar wisdoms running contrary to commonsense.

Newcomers and new ideas are always suspect. Intruders find that every searching stare of village folk is barbed with enquiry. These same faces confronted in the routine course of the day are noticeably etched with unbroken lineage. Time stopped here in the twelfth century or thereabouts when Saxons and Normans found good reason for wanting to stay. Hardly surprising then that these are private people who defy the passing stranger to trespass beyond surface contact. Their ancestors possess the churchyard with immemorial right. It is their ancient ground marking their family histories and asserting that their forebears hold its green antiquity in common tenure. One is left in no doubt that their dead are a material presence guarding a shadowy freehold in perpetuity for living kith and kin. And why not? They might, with good cause, claim they were about when the Vikings were weighing up the local prospects and have been around ever since. In such circumstances it hardly seems prudent to question village rights. This changelessness of local life proclaims its certainties in granite monuments. Men determined to outlive time do it in style. Faith chiselled into the rock of ages never forgets its gods.

Restless urban life is not for them; it is too transient. Two World Wars are still part of living memory. The sons, the village cheered on to Flanders, are still flesh and blood to generations that never saw them go. People will linger in public places to yarn and spin their legends. The years and a changing world cannot alter that. The pace of village minds contracts time into easy, discursive days. Less cohesive communities are quick to weary and pleased to forget. Here folk know that out there, beyond the weathered thatch of their slow haven, the speed of life trivialises mens' beliefs, cheapens attitudes and drains a man's pride.

Newcomers are resented as intruders if they appear to want to stay, but tolerated if visiting and passing through. Visitors are welcome to treat themselves to home-baked scones and clotted cream. A villager will never scorn a well earned penny. Intruders, that buy village property, remain strangers who tart up houses for holiday use or dispose of for quick profit. Those that stay to die are allowed to share a privileged tenancy in the churchyard under the summoning bells of the Norman tower. Strangers cannot expect to gain acceptance among the village-living in the course of a single lifetime. That is too brief a span for home-grown folk to come to terms with an outsider's soul, but dying here creates a bond of sorts. No-one beyond the parish can purchase eternity in the churchyard. Parish death begins the breakdown of 'non-acceptability'. Dying here admits the stranger to the pantheon of village immortals. Then local judgement becomes easy truth and makes its peace with the departed.

Until recent times, daily experience threw up no perplexities for the parish – it takes its norms in life from God. No question here that he alone holds the rational nature of existence in lofty, holy comprehension. In cases of difficulty or strife, one negotiates with the Almighty. The church is open seven days a week for just that. Furthermore God exempts villagers from all obligations towards strangers and each man sets down his own terms – you take them or be damned!

The only outward sign of circumstantial change hereabouts during the last hundred years turns on the dying of the village's trading heart. Once the horse was work, power and freedom to rural folk and three thriving smithies testified to that. With the coming of the internal combustion engine and its devilish offspring, the horseless carriage, the smithies closed one by one. The last survivor struggled on repairing lawn mowers, bicycles and Model T Fords until he too sold up and moved out. The most regretted loss was the family butcher, still remembered as a craftsman with a surgeon's skill, whose eye for good meat was legendary. His shop on the green is now a pink-wash private dwelling.

The general store struggles on and still offers its good-natured **threshold to a community seduced by the impulsive distractions of car** shopping and supermarket convenience. Weekends and holidays reaffirm old-time village values as forgetful housewives creep gratefully across the green to that handy oasis for a pound of sugar (perish the metric!) or a packet of marg.

THE POWER BROKERS

In recent times the outside world has invaded village awareness with the glamour of things lumped under the banner of 'progress'. Regional planning, now headline copy, has wreaked its influences, exciting credulous minds and promoting a surge of restlessness for change. Furthermore, and this is fair comment, much local thinking has been contaminated by policies hatched in committee 'strong -rooms' at District and County levels. There will always be a vocal lobby, ever ready to be swept on to folly by the enthusiasm of others – especially if the others are lionised as local born and bred leaders or *progressives* looked up to as providers of distraction from the kind of boredom many people find inherent in the *status quo*. Since it requires some insight into how individuals or groups make decisions in the realms of planning politics, this last potent psychological factor escapes the interested enquiry it deserves.

We are led to believe that inside their bureaucratic fortresses, planners are using wisdom and integrity as far as commercial interests and population trends are concerned. In dealing with national needs, they rely on promoting regional industrial growth and population migration. Yet increasingly, the outcome appears to ignore the considerations of environmental uniqueness, apart from those areas already embraced by concerned organisations like the National Trust. Needless to say, the contrary is repeatedly protested at planning top level. Inexplicably, the term 'unique' has no place in the vocabulary of these people. If it had, surviving rural communities and their villages, would by now have been designated national treasures like works of art and protected by special planning privileges. Let us protest the point more vehemently: we must secure complete protection against any development that does not meet the most stringent needs and apply the most sensitive aesthetic standards.

Thus their subversive notion *progress* digs in to unsettle the timeless order. Even when it appears to be resented, paraded commercial benefits quickly cushion village resentment.

The village wisemen talked of reviving village trade, when no shops remained unconverted into private houses and the magnetic draw of the supermarket, a short distance away, was recognised as irresistible. Yet their arguments ignore this. It does not take parochial reasoning too long to reconcile all its illogicalities. With the question of insight out of the way, sane judgement is excused duty.

The affairs of villages hereabouts, once gently concerned with harvests, immemorial country fairs and fêtes are todays cauldrons of ambition. Most people are only too happy to declare themselves 'otherwise engaged' when it comes to community business. In the midst of this parochial sloth, activists wearing Napoleon's mantle emerge to map their grand strategies and many a village green becomes a Moscow against which they fling their pretentious armies of driving ambition. Then irrationally, what the bystanders once regarded as sacred, immutable and right, is trodden under foot in a Gadarene rush to go for the new. No chance now for ageless order and rural perfection. There is certainly no glory in the mellow antiquity of cob and thatch. Today's urban politics decrees that golden crowns are far more likely to be found on the mega-store shelves of giant shopping precincts. Top local people plot change, oblivious of the fact that in ancient settled environments, all change blights. Of course this view is hotly disputed in many quarters. Even worse, when events prove the fact, blatant evidence is just as hotly denied!

Those of us who flee the madding crowd, usually stand on vantage points of wider and sadder personal experiences. Left to despair, we find ourselves vainly trying to protect what others despise or fail to value. Loving the countryside is akin to having religion, for its truths are eternal. Its mysteries and contemplative graces endure when all else is found to be worthless. When it suffers loss or despoilation, its lovers grieve. We balance the knowledge of a world increasingly over-exploited by man against his failure to protect its life supporting capabilities. Ultimately we stand to pay dearly for this failure for when time stops on earth, there is nowhere else for man to go.

LOCAL PLANNING HISTORY

The Council archives, covering the previous two decades, had disclosed one or two planning submissions flirting with the notion that part of the valley nearest the village should be released to housing.

Indeed a small group of council dwellings was built in the early nineteen fifties on the immediate fringe of the village, unobtrusively under the lea of the hills, without trespassing the landscape. Today it can be rightly judged as the last development offering no scenic threat to the valley. Subsequently all major schemes were allowed to lapse. The village was isolated, lacking amenities and served by difficult roads.

In private it was generally agreed that any further encroachment would set a precedent in planning likely to burst the floodgates. Such a course was certain to leave no part of the region safe, although that consideration was not regarded as more than a side issue by certain long-standing members of the Parish Council. Councillors spent much discussion time convincing themselves that marriages and births in the village were straining housing demands to breaking point, although the facts denied this (see later).

During this period the village rejected a proposal to be designated a conservation area. Local opposition was convinced, quite wrongly, that such a move would encase the parish in onerous restrictive covenants affecting every householder, e.g. individuals would lose the right to determine the external colour of their own houses, even their own front doors! Listed dwellings are subject to such restrictions, but they would be in any rural or city location. Council leaders, who knew better, did nothing to dispel these fears. But more of that later in the chapter elaborating on the machinations of council politics.

To the north east of the valley one artifact, the abandoned and derelict railway line to Esturville (closed in the post- Beeching era), remained a realistic route for future road links. County planners duly sited the north-west passage of the recently opened County Bypass along its course.

Happily for Patfield Moor a proposal to construct a linking slip-road to the village was priced out of the scheme, though many parishioners felt cheated by this loss. Meanwhile the population in general remains optimistically delighted by, or numbly resigned to, or ignorantly oblivious of the wide-ranging impact the road was to have on this corner of the county. In particular how its existence would put pressure on the planning intentions of adjoining councils and business interests. Now we had a major preoccupation – how to exploit the bypass-gain to enrich the region through acceptable tourism. Less

IN A CONCESSION TO ENVIRONMENTALISTS THE CHAIRMAN'S WIFE UNVEILS THE NEW WILDLIFE TUNNEL UNDER THE NEW ROAD

acceptable to the enlightened, given the pristine rolling farmlands of the region now at risk, are extensive house building schemes, hi- tech industry and intensified commerce. Conveniently the planners appeared to have ignored the obvious fact that tourism demands, in great measure, the scenic satisfaction of unblemished countryside. Ignored too was the immemorial industry of the region — farming. This emerald county offers some of the richest farmland in Britain. Disturbingly, our county policy makers appear to be moving towards vitiating this great planet-friendly industry (we stick with this descriptive notwithstanding farming's recently much publicised record of careless attitudes towards environmental pollution).

LOCAL MEGA-DOOM

Following the government's (sometimes) laudable insistence on progressive relaxation of planning restrictions, the scene was set in this rural backwater, to unleash forces hellbent on transforming a sleepy country haven into an intensively developed regional community. We were told that the interests of the growing indigenous population was mainly being addressed here. Seen by business minds as a bright new dawn, it became enshrined in futuristic language, worthy of Hollywood's flamboyant style — 'North County 2001' Rejingo'd, this read to the wise — 'North County Urban Jungle 2001'!

Certainly there was no shyness about the thrust of the plan, for it was patently land hungry. The house building target was set above 70,000 new homes. All villages and hamlets were to be considered for expansion. 'Infill' and 'reschedule' became the buzz words in the scamper for sites.

Furthermore it became increasingly apparent that nothing was sacred; beauty, scale, style and history were uncommercial — out of date and out of fashion! It disclosed a pit of insensitive thinking. It opened to horrified observers' eyes the depths of local planning opinions' negative values. We heard, with disbelief, landscapes of surpassing loveliness dismissed as weed patches. Every land owner, big and small, saw their precious parcels of greensward transformed into goldfields. In this respect many of us would stand condemned!

However, the gluttonous approval of land exploitation and instant wealth was not confined to the possessors. Villagers hereabouts are not overtly covetous and in any event inter-relationships spread wide and are deep rooted. The chances are a Bloggs married a Brown in the last century and now everyone in the parish is a cousin of some remove. This happy conjunction ensures that families move along a hybrid conveyor belt of rosy inheritance.

Rumour usually anticipates fact in close communities. Before the mandatory announcement appeared in the local press public sector advertisement columns, we all knew that a major event was hatching. Individuals purported to have financial stakes in the fate of the valley were already ensconced in the local hostelry entertaining each other royally in happy expectation of their certain bonanza, one they were convinced was as good as in their pockets (public bar gossip).

5

THE BATTLE TO SAVE THE VALLEY

The village was hotly divided over the leaked details.

As we have described, indigenous villagers are traditionally resentful towards newcomers. It is easy to appreciate how this tends to consolidate sentiment behind their own kith and kin, whatever the merits of the business in hand. Purposeful discussion is notoriously difficult in village politics unless consensus moves it. Here, in the main, consensus lines up behind family or group interest.

The points listed below summarise the arguments in favour of exploiting the valley. Although expressing the views held by the village pro-development lobby, they also reflect unresearched parochial amenity needs, as perceived by many villagers who held no brief for schemes violating the valley. We offer them to set the scene for this stage of the narrative.

◆ The village needs to grow to remain viable.

◆ It lacks starter homes and denies the legitimate expectations and aspirations of the village young wishing to set up home among family and friends.

◆ It needs car parking facilities and childrens' play areas.

◆ It needs sports facilities for football and cricket.

◆ It needs small industry.

◆ More children are needed to anticipate falling attendance at the local school.

◆ At all costs it must avoid becoming a retirement village.

Ironically population trends nationwide support the fact that the birth rate is falling. It is not tenable to contend that small communities can grow through self-generated expansion of existing families. Inevitably local populations must seek to grow at the expense of near or distant communities. The chances are, since the population is also aging, most villages will, in due course, become places of retirement. This invalidates the last contention given above.

Since these arguments do not stand condemned on their own merit, except for the last one already dealt with, each point will be taken up again as it arises in the course of the narrative. What emerges will prove that no matter how reasonable stated 'facts' seems to be, when they are properly investigated and analysed within prevailing social amenities, those same facts become pretentious fictions.

HOUSING REQUIREMENTS

We begin by taking the most strenuously argued point concerning need for new homes. There appeared to be no serious research into the village's alleged lack of available houses and nobody at any level of planning tabled the question – what shortage ?

When the points above were being hotly debated, there were twelve unsold, low-priced cottages on offer in the village. Did the parish really need unsympathetic new houses of very basic utilitarian design? This point bears emphasis because the need stressed was for low-cost housing, only possible if all the specifications were bottom-of-the-market-affordable. Today we know that this means skimped and characterless. Submitted plans later confirmed this. There is a hard-to-explain sentiment among the young couples in the village that new is beautiful. We do not necessarily quarrel with this view, but as we have repeatedly said, ancient villages need to cling to their antiquity. Unless very sensitively and expensively designed, modern buildings invariably destroy the character and charm of old settlements.

Without addressing the known reality of the housing market, the village leaders persisted with their sanctimonious rhetoric, emphasising a phony and chronic shortage of low-cost housing for young families.

We started with rumour, but in the end, all our speculative fears proved to be well founded. Though it was said the proposals designated low-cost houses, housing associations were not involved. Several major building companies were hinted at as putative developers, all of whom either built expensively to a high specification, or worse still, densely and badly to a low specification.

Some of the reputations of the suggested developers cast doubt on their commercial probity. Several were known, from past planning histories, to exploit reasonable planning approval to increase agreed densities under threat of costly appeals they could afford to finance. Recent regional planning disputes have added a disturbing catalogue of such cases, confirming that this odious practice is on the increase. Defending councils, finding their own resources heavily stretched, are in a weak position to offer effective resistance.

Because there is no way that first-time buyers can be isolated and targeted, it is inevitable that the normal forces of the market are free to take over. New owners cannot be prevented, subsequently, from exploiting the inflationary house market. Thus new properties inevitably get removed from the low-cost spectrum.

However, some hope exists as new flexibility in the Government's planning guidelines offers a way of building new rural homes at affordable prices. The terms of sale, if properly applied, ensuring that when sold they remain at low cost to local people forever. Unfortunately, it is still possible for a commercial developer to set up a 'housing association' which is one in name only. While it has the low cost component, the other benefits are missing and the fact that they are making a profit in circumstances where this is repudiated, is shrewdly hidden. Very searching questions have to be asked about any scheme offered to a community where there is a link with a commercial organisation.

Finally on this matter, several approved infill sites remain undeveloped in unobtrusive corners of the village. No opposition to their being used for housing was going to be raised. At this point we feel we can leave the other important questions listed above. They arise again in the course of the narrative together with their answers and are best left to fall naturally into the perspectives of this little history.

THE DEVELOPER'S PLANS

The farmer owning the valley land engaged a local planning consultant reputed to have a good track-record in planning successes. He

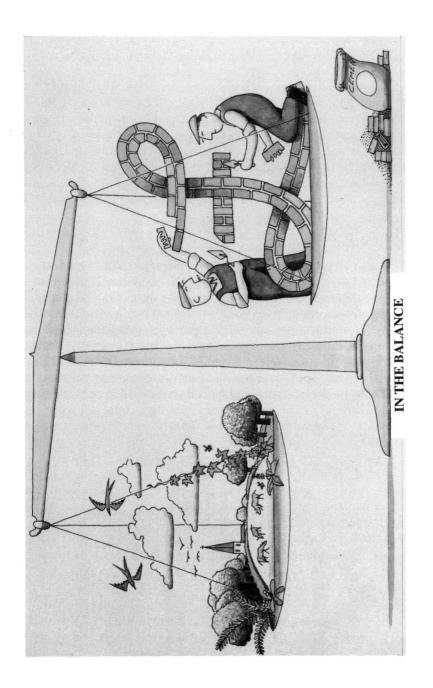

IN THE BALANCE

produced an extensive scheme to put a thirty-house-development in the valley. This was duly submitted for District Council planning consent.

To give the development social and moral credibility, seven of the planned houses were hypocritically described as 'starter homes'. Later this was acknowledged as misleading. Only then did it become a public fact that there was no intention on the developer's part to involve housing associations, whose charters solely and specifically tie-in the houses built under their aegis as starter homes for all time.

However, a disconcerting bait that was hooked to the scheme, addressed two of the previously mentioned pressing village needs:

◆ A site for recreation facilities.
◆ Car parks.

These would not be a gift to the village in return for planning consent, but would only be made available for as long as the villagers proved the need, i.e. by use and maintainance. The parish was to bear the cost and responsibility.

The issue of recreational facilities put a revealing spotlight on the sporting history of the village. Years ago it had a thriving football and cricket team using village land privately leased to them at peppercorn rents. However, when the landlord refused to maintain the pitches to the required standard, passing responsibility for such maintainance back to the sporting members, the clubs promptly disbanded. The effort involved was simply not congenial to the membership!

Car parking in the village has been a problem for many years. The layout of the village centre goes back to feudal times; it is rigidly constrained by ancient land usage. A family garage is a rarity and street-parking the rule. Our parish councillors, whilst accepting the limited number of parking spaces offered by the planning consultant's gesture, nevertheless made it clear that they would use the availability of free parking spaces to network the village roads with yellow lines and impose the authority of a traffic warden. A police notice advising against street parking was circulated about this time but no advice was offered as to how this could be achieved. Readers are alerted to this type of local authoritarian thinking. Furthermore, could people be persuaded to park their cars out of view of their homes, especially given todays increasing risk of vandalism ?

CONSEQUENCES BEGIN TO EMERGE

The first families to be effectively threatened by the proposals were those whose houses faced across the valley. The measure of the threat was perceived in very real terms. Ten thousand pounds was knocked off the price of one cottage currently up for sale! The selling agent, ruefully admitting that the beauty of the existing view was its greatest asset.

HITTING BACK

By word of mouth people affected by or opposed to the scheme made their sentiments known to each other and a meeting was convened at the home of the couple whose house was to suffer the dramatic devaluation described above. We determined that action was important and wasted little time on abusing a rotten scheme or commiserating with unfortunate new friends.

We formed the Patfield Moor Environmental Protection Society (P.E.P.S.). This gave us group identity and credibility. Professional status of committee members is also beneficial. People's perception of doctors as responsible and clear-sighted members of the community still holds sway in the public domain. We must say, not unkindly, that the snob factor in society means that having a member of a profession in your group enhances your standing in these situations. Whether social esteem for members of learned professions is merited or not, a doctor in our ranks served us well when dealing with the media.

The first meeting of P.E.P.S. was business-like. Officers were appointed:
1. Chairman.
2. Clerk.
3. Treasurer.

The meeting was minuted and the clerk, in due course, produced well-typed copies. A good typist is a great help. The luxury of a word processor appears to be indispensable today.

SUPPORT GAINED

P.E.P.S. circulated the entire parish with an invitation to a prior meeting at the church assembly rooms. Its purpose was to gauge the sentiments of a greater representative village gathering. It also offered a better chance to recruit more opposition to the scheme in less regimented circumstances. We considered it good politics, besides being relaxing, to begin the campaign by organising a wider audience of potential sympathisers without the intimidating presence of any official personalities. We hoped to create a climate in which even reticent villagers could give free expression to their views, wishes and fears. It was treated like a dress rehearsal to the real thing.

Note: The public are not allowed to speak at ordinary parish council meetings; the exception to this rule hinges on a parishioner advising the parish clerk, in writing, twenty-four hours before a scheduled meeting, that he or she wishes to raise a given matter in the period allocated to any other business (more of that point below).

Rumour had it that the chairman of the Parish Council had declared our meeting illegal, since it was his stated prerogative to chair all such meetings called in the parish. We ignore this. But take note: our parish politicians claim this as a protocol privilege, although we doubt that it is enforceable or indeed legal.

Our 'illegal' meeting was attended by fifty parishioners, which P.E.P.S. members felt constituted a high level of public concern.

It is highly unlikely that you will go forward on a tide of popular consensus. However worthy your cause, entrenched opinion, found in all communities, will quickly surface and express its resentment. Expect to be harassed; your opponents will be neither fair nor rational in their prejudices and hostility. All differences will be exploited. As our chairman entered the meeting, he was handed an oblique 'death threat' With the accusation that P.E.P.S. members were 'a load of cockney foreigners', (a local euphamism for outsiders, c.f. NIMBYS), came the assertion that 'the only good cockney was a dead one'! We relate this episode, not because we treated it seriously, but to show the degree of malice that can be aroused in these circumstances. It had to be seen as a personal attack on the chairman and one or two founding members of P.E.P.S., rather than blanket criticism of the assembled protesters, most of whom were recognisable as old inhabitants of the village, who could claim long historic connections to the region. This group quickly made it clear that they valued the uniqueness of the valley with the same passionate concern as the more recent residents. All the attending public were solidly against the 'rape' of our countryside, a term used increasingly to express the depth of feeling now aroused among perceptive and concerned villagers.

A resolution was passed to request the Parish Council chairman to call a Parish Meeting to discuss the future of the valley and take a public vote on submitted plans. It is the chairman's prerogative to decide on this course of action, but if he displays reluctance to do so, parishioners can force the issue by petitioning for such a meeting. This requires a petition carrying not less than six parishioners' signatures. The petition must be addressed to the Parish Council and duly handed to the Parish Council clerk. It is not a bad thing to deliver this kind of document by hand rather than trusting it to the post, when this is feasible. It avoids giving the powers that be an excuse to delay matters by asserting that it did not arrive or was delayed.

Our forward-planning strategy drew this further conclusion:

In the build up to this vital event, it was important that widespread awareness of the issues involved had to be aroused. Protesting demands that one gets in first to spread the word. In this way one can increase the impact of what is at stake on ones own terms and highlight it. This key factor requires you to explain yourselves clearly and design your campaign protocol to gain as much sympathy as possible.

APPROACH TO THE MEDIA

P.E.P.S. now launched a full-scale campaign to make the matter a regional issue. We began by attempting to engage the attention of this wider audience by utilising local and regional press and television. Both these branches of public communication will respond to controversy if its social value is high.

If one succeeds in addressing a much wider audience, it becomes even more vital to see that your case is clearly outlined and presented with intelligent concern. Distant onlookers are likely to be dismissive of your campaign if you cannot show them that your issues could have serious and far-reaching implications.

We advised earlier not to let emotions run riot when promoting your case, but arguments can be forcibly presented if it is appropriate to do so. Forcefulness, untainted by irrational rhetoric, can impress the public in righteous debate.

The television editorial response was encouraging and soon proved positive. A news team, headed by a well-known presenter, made contact and duly agreed to film our group in a protest interview.

A good rule is to choose one of your members to be spokesperson. We selected our representative on the merits of being:

◆ A lucid speaker with a knack of coming straight to the point.

◆ Good at countering opposition arguments especially when confronted by a sharp inquisitor.

◆ Well versed in your cause with an agreeable manner.

To allow self-opinionated colleagues to covet the limelight without regard to their ability to impress others by handling your case well, will prejudice a major public relations opportunity and could jeopardise the entire campaign. In campaigning for a good cause, every member of the group should regard his or her role with objective humility.

In the event, the television team displayed encouraging sympathy towards us. The presenter approved of our cause, recognising the environmental threat to the valley.

It seems that most informed members of society are responsive to sensitive environmental issues. It was encouraging to realise we were on common ground with our interviewer when he took us through a rehearsal.

Television current affairs crews want to achieve a hard-hitting, topical feature and will help rather than hinder if the matter in hand is relevant, justified and urgent; even better if it has a wide regional appeal. The presenter will often play devil's advocate but only to enhance the interest of your case. We did not feel at any time that we were being boxed in for the sake of exposing weaknesses or creating sensational journalism. Finally, when the programme was broadcast – few of them are relayed live – the editing proved fair and appropriate. Subsequent feedback indicated we had achieved our purpose and consolidated sympathy for our fight. Remember, your opponents will be given the right to reply in the same slot. Do not be upset or surprised if your views are vehemently opposed and those expressing them given generous screen time. Expect to see the television crew roaming the district for other interviewees when they have done with you.

PARISH MEETING CALLED

The Parish Council chairman agreed to hold an open parish meeting. Again P.E.P.S. appointed a spokesperson, but we all agreed, that in line with traditional practice, everyone could have their say should events justify. The village hall was filled to capacity and standing room barely provided enough space to accommodate the crowd.

It was soon evident that we had strangers in our midst. The farmer making the planning application had mustered many friends from outside the parish boundary. But the sinister purpose of this move was not evident until voting on the planning motion took place. The ebb and flow of the dispute, much of which expounded familiar and mostly untenable arguments in favour of development, finally led to a hand-count majority decision to reject the scheme in its presented form. This left the applicant free to re-present an amended proposal. He and his planning consultant quit the meeting satisfied that they had split the sympathies of the village. They also had the encouragement of being armed with a mandate to come back to planning with a scheme of different density. Changed in form but not in intention!

This decision left most of us appalled. We all recognised that the result was engineered by voters from outside the parish but our protests were brushed aside. Our chairman brazenly stated that he knew the faces of all his 'flock' and had taken the 'alien' factor into account. No one could challenge this apart from demanding a fresh secret ballot vote; it emphasised the weaknesses of taking decisions on hand-counts. There seemed every reason to believe that the Parish Council was committed to unbridled village expansion and was taking little care to disguise the fact.

It is surprising how pessimistic one can become after such an encounter! But remember – the opening shots fired in every campaign do not decide the outcome of the battle.

Advice: Since an open meeting of this nature is important and can highlight unexpected consequences, such as those we have just related, it is perfectly reasonable to arm yourself with the presence of a responsible observer from a higher authority. District or County

Council members are quite receptive to invitations to attend constituency meetings. They will obviously not comment at the time, but any irregularities encountered will be kept in the forefront of their thinking and indeed the likelihood of improprieties taking place in their presence will be minimised.

PETITIONING

Our next defensive move was concerned with convincing the people in the District Council planning department that a site meeting was not only imperative, but a vital part of making all members involved in taking the final decision view the destructive consequences of the planned development. We began petitioning parish councillors verbally and in writing to achieve this end.

In due course, the planning application was placed on the agenda of the District Council Planning Committee and in the meanwhile P.E.P.S. sent a deputation to its chairman. Then, as a follow-up, a further stream of letters was addressed to all the members of the District Council Planning Committee both paid and elected. Again it must be emphasised that titles and responsibilities must be clearly identified and acknowledged.

MEETING THE DISTRICT CHAIRMAN

The planning committee chairman was courteous and appeared sympathetic, but made great capital out of the Government's directive to all councils to be as unobstructive as possible when dealing with applications for housing development. He was emphatic that councils today had little option but to toe the Whitehall line, however sensitive the environmental issues were. Nevertheless, he said he did not personally like the scheme and felt that there was every chance of it being blocked. This belief was overshadowed by the chance interruption of our interview by another elected member of the committee who expressed, in no uncertain terms, her contempt for most of the local rural landscape. Whenever exchanged views drew attention to our wonderful beauty spot, she responded by saying 'I've seen better'. Finally she openly welcomed the scheme and said 'We need to build in the valley.' We record this to underline the spectrum of opinions and outlook one will encounter in the course of planning disputes.

It is difficult at these moments not to view most members encountered in planning departments as insensitive to all aspects of rural beauty and rural values. Notwithstanding pressing community housing needs and vital local industrial and commercial growth, it is still depressing to realise that the choice between exploitation and preservation is still the issue. Since the countryside appeared severely handicapped in this contest, we concluded it had no chance.

THE DISTRICT COUNCIL PLANNING MEETING

P.E.P.S. members were present in the public gallery.

At last we were being given our chance to assess private views and arguments aired in public. We felt one conviction was proved: our Parish Council Chairman doubling as Vice-chairman of the District Council Planning Committee wanted the valley scheme to go ahead. When challenged later he fiercely refuted this, arguing that his attitude was necessary to pave the way for an eventual site meeting, 'which you all want'. Since we were unaware of planning protocol, which would have insisted on this anyway given the strength of the opposition to the scheme, we gave him the benefit of doing his honest best in the light of committee experience.

But at the conclusion of the discussion the site meeting was finally agreed upon because:

◆ The depth of opposition in the parish was sufficiently great to justify the demand that it be held.

◆ The professional officers recommended refusal on multifactorial grounds; these were surprisingly relevant and unexpected (see later).

We left the council chambers highly encouraged, but were warned that the case could go against us at the site meeting. Professional opinion is often overturned when judgement is tossed into the unpredictable arena of on-site debate.

The experience of one look is worth a thousand words and drawings, but unfortunately this is no safeguard in planning disputes. Even the most righteous causes can fall foul of determined lobbying from skillfully briefed pressure groups. Experts are well paid to raise the stakes in favour of the partisan interests they are retained to represent. One cannot fail to admire the way in which speculators parade their schemes as fulfilling social needs. End decisions so often contradict the logic of conservation, even when no arguments can be advanced to justify ecological destruction. Do not give up. Prepare yourselves well and do not be overcome by hopelessness or succumb to cynicism.

We heard this parting statement voiced among the committee as it wound up its business: 'This issue will not go away'. This was a sentiment that appeared to underscore our belief that the development lobby would hammer away at business until they got the approval they sought.

THE END GAME

P.E.P.S. convened to plan a massed show of strength on the day of the site meeting. Since the valley was now to be visually evaluated for the first time, the moment had arrived to highlight its scenic and environmental uniqueness. We were not prepared to see these given short shift by the 'blind', however aggressively they were prepared to promote the development lobby. We first listed the arguments that had determined our case from the beginning:

◆ The need to defend the sanctity of the valley because of its unspoilt, pristine beauty.

◆ The valley's environmental fragility. The clean flowing river. Its abundant wildlife. Rich seasonal displays of wild rural flora. The great variety of healthy trees. The rightness of the village itself within the overall, undamaged picture. (The list could be endless.)

◆ The significance of the village, in this overexploited age, as an irreplaceable, unchanged feudal relic framed by an ancient landscape. How can we claim to have high moral purpose, if we are not prepared to defend our history against the appetites of our times ? We say 'show us irrefutable need before destroying the past and its place in the natural world'.

Other reasons already touched upon in the text became our basis of more emphatic comment.

The village has few rural industries outside farming. Its shops, apart from the general store and post office, had closed in the face of competition from the great supermarkets. An excellent private bus service and the car had brought every conceivable service and utility, including medical centres, within easy reach.

We aimed to present ourselves as we truly were — concerned parishioners sharing the environmental anxieties of our time — and certainly not driven by petty and selfish motives. Nor did we envy the applicant farmer who was, after all, a neighbour who until this issue had arisen was treated evenly on terms of friendship.

We proposed to incorporate some of our views on well-designed placards. Our intention was to stage a high profile but orderly demonstration. We again contacted the local press and television.

As the village boasts an active art group, we thought it might heighten interest and assist credibility if we arranged a mass painting event, 'Our Environment as a Work of Art'. One of our members went further and constructed a large metal sculpture in the form of a dancing ballerina entitled *Spirit of the Valley*.

A directive from the Chairman of the District Council Planning Committee, advised us that only one spokesperson was allowed to speak for P.E.P.S. We chose the colleague who had spoken so well for us during the television programme a few weeks earlier. Remember the site meeting establishes the 'end stage' of the matter. Decisions, favourable or adverse, are made then. If they go against you, the stark tedium of a last-resort-appeal becomes reality.

THE SITE MEETING

The day was promisingly fine. On such a fortunate day the countryside spoke for itself. Events took shape more or less as planned. A television crew was on hand and the local press sent photographers. Our placards made factual points and though paraded prominently, inflamatory attitudes and gestures were avoided. Aggression in public protest always looks ugly, however passionately one feels about the objectives. It invariably comes across as antisocial, always threatens violence and when this erupts matters disintegrate and you stand to lose what you have set out to win. Flashpoints are always present in protest situations. Later the violence is remembered when the cause is forgotten.

Fighting the Developers

Eight professional people attended comprising paid members of the District Council Planning Department, representatives from public utilities, i.e. water and electricity, and members of the Highways Department. All of these incidentally put their characteristic 'blots' into every landscape they touch. The District Council planning chairman took charge of the proceedings and set the rules. Our Parish Council chairman busied about actively lobbying. Our spokesperson was nominated and accepted by the meeting. The District Council chairman outlined the planning application.

In agreed order the case for and against the scheme was put by the villagers. The architect representing the applicant was an articulate advocate. He was given a generous hearing. Parish Councillors were also invited to make their case and most favoured the development.

Finally, when all lay opinions had been fairly aired, the professional members gave the 'core arguments' which duly damned the application . These are now summarised:

◆ Sewage capacity of the village was already at full stretch. If the scheme was approved the developers would have to install a new sewage system capable of taking all the sewage of the village, including the increased volume generated by the new housing estate. It would have been a major capital undertaking and it was made clear that the developers would have to absorb the costs. This was estimated to be in region of £500,000. Simple arithmetic will show the unit-cost-increase house prices would have to absorb in turn.

◆ Thirty new homes, according to the Highways Authority, would generate a further traffic flow of 240 vehicles per day and the road system within the village, however redesigned, would not cope.

◆ The proposed development was considered poorly related to the village and at variance with the County Structure Plan.

◆ Since the site was considered to be in an area of great landscape value, it was felt that the development would be of detriment to the region.

◆ There was some criticism of inadequate footpaths and poorly sited car parks within the overall design of the complex. There appeared to be no scope in the scheme to remedy this fault − nor was it possible.

◆ Part of the site floods in severe weather conditions.

◆ The ruling given below refers to the existing road serving the small group of council houses (now tenant owned) earlier described

THIS EXCHANGE ACTUALLY TOOK PLACE IN PATFIELD MOOR

as lying under the lea of the hills bounding the valley. This road could possibly have provided access to the proposed housing estate. Certainly its course ran directly to the planned site. The reason given for rejecting its suitability provides an interesting precedent and a powerful line of protest enquiry when questions of existing road access to sites under threat are raised.

The local Highway Authorities ruling concerning acceptable standards that enable roads and footpaths to be adopted was given. The access road, in this instance, constituted a private *street*, designed, it would seem at the time of construction, to serve a small self-limiting development. This did not conform to standards necessary to allow adoption. To aprove it would therefore go against the advice contained in the Department of the Environments circular 79/74.

With the formalities of the site meeting over, the District Council members and the officers deliberated in camera. Finally, when the chairman appeared to announce the verdict, he advised that the scheme had been overwhelmingly rejected! Our weeks of effort were over and our tenacity to the cause of saving the valley was vindicated.

At the subsequent District Council meeting, where the matter was scheduled for discussion at full committee level, it was disclosed that the developer, on behalf of the applicant, had withdrawn the application.

We later learned that no appeal was planned. The scheme had been dropped!

CAMPAIGN ADVICE

Keeping Briefed

◆ When important events are threatened, never ignore or dismiss taproom gossip, church fete small talk and insider 'know-all' leaks. Remember, in local community politics, all smoke denotes fire.

◆ Never fail to read the public notices in the local press.

◆ Whenever possible, attend Parish or District Council meetings. It is a citizen's inalienable right to do so and all local matters will be disclosed. Furthermore the performance of your elected representatives can be monitored, assessed and judged (c.f. next election prospects).

◆ Every interested individual is allowed access to all District Council planning documents and these are always freely available for inspection in their planning departments.

◆ Do not be myopic or xenophobic. Keep informed about neighbouring village affairs. They often mirror ones own problems and disputes and provide valuable guidance in the diplomacy and management of your-own-doorstep business. Read local press correspondence columns. They are indispensable hives of useful chatter, comment, opinion and predictions!

HISTORICAL NOTE:

In February 1960 Margaret Thatcher, then a back bench M.P., presented the 'Public Bodies (Admission of the Press to Meetings) Bill' to the House of Commons. The main aim of the Bill was to bring committee, as well as council meetings, within the provisions of the Act and compel local authorities to release agendas in advance of all council meetings.

The Bill in its emergent form achieved, in some measure, the intention of creating more open local government. Councils and committees still have the right of exclusion when they deem that matters prejudicial to the public interest are being discussed.

Comment:

Today citizens may well ask by what right is any issue concerning the daily life of people entitled to be judged as being prejudicial to public interest. Secrecy in all matters of government, whether local or national, is under healthy attack. Unceasing vigilance and citizen involvement will help make its demise absolute.

CAMPAIGN ADVICE

How to Conduct your Group

◆ Keeping accurate records of every transaction is essential; this includes letters, whoever in the group writes them. Preferably all mail-shots should be committee adjudicated. Word processors ensure that this task imposes few burdens.

◆ Avoid personal attacks.

◆ Be objective and civil.

◆ Do not flirt with libellous matter however provocative the circumstances.

◆ Adopt a strict convention in all your transactions of keeping precisely to the business in hand. It is difficult among friends in socially congenial surroundings, but do persist in trying to maintain this discipline nevertheless.

◆ In dealing with unacceptably sited developments, explore constructive alternatives, e.g. unused land sites, situated in less sensitive local areas, might be available for the proposed developments under review and could solve the problems. Remember the issue will sooner or later enjoy a wide ranging public debate and arming yourselves with in-depth knowledge of land availability will immeasurably strengthen your authority to challenge bad schemes.

◆ Agree resolutions for extra-mural action (e.g. personal lobbying and group protesting) and delegate members to attend to them.

GOLDEN RULES

Psychological Factors

Rule 1. Know what you are opposing.

Rule 2. Know in the wider context of village or urban politics, who supports you and who opposes you.

Rule 3. Be aware that those who oppose you are generally prepared to go to greater lengths in fighting you than your friends are in supporting you.

Rule 4. Get to know your opponents' personal qualities, their motives, their public reputations, their past record and their philosophy of life. This is not so ridiculous as it first reads. Locally we are aware of certain men dominating our politics, who see themselves as men of destiny searching for bigger kingdoms. It is a fact of life that politics and power are indivisibly linked. The position of Parish Chairman is something of a dead end for the ambitious local politician. It offers few rewards when compared to the noble office of town mayor. Armed with civic achievements, those attaining this latter position could reasonably expect to retire from office with a royal accolade. We are not suggesting that today's villages can be made into towns, although historic evidence proves that this has happened. Nevertheless, inside every parochial power seeker, there burns the the need to enlarge his or her sphere of dominance. Do not doubt that this may be the invincible parochial force you are up against, in its drive for expression.

CAMPAIGN ACTION

Practicalities

◆ Study the submitted plans at District Council Offices. Take note: all plans are copyright. No photocopies are allowed. A resourceful member of your group should be able to produce a reasonably readable sketch; this will give us some insight into planning intentions. From the day the plans are announced in the press, usually the local journal, two weeks' grace is allowed to lodge objections.

◆ Attend in force when the next Parish Council is convened to discuss the planning application. It cannot be over stressed that the Parish Council, though not a major voice, is at higher levels taken as reflecting the will of parishioners. It is powerfully persuasive when not challenged. Ignore it at your peril.

◆ The Local Government Act 1972 requires councils to arrange for minutes to be open for inspection by the public free of charge at reasonable hours. These must have been approved and signed by the chairman. There is no legal obligation to make available unconfirmed minutes but many councils circulate these with the agenda before a meeting. Ask yourselves if you are getting this service from your council; if not, take appropriate steps to enforce this courtesy.

◆ Get a list of all the elected and professional members of the District Council planning department.

◆ Compile a list of valid objections, condense them into polite, concise, unemotive letters and flood your targeted councillors with them. Be sure to address the letters properly, i.e. get the names, initials, titles, honours, positions and functions correct. Nothing outrages a man more than when people give him an M.B.E. after the Queen has honoured him with an O.B.E., or addresses him as an ordinary committee member when, in fact, he is the chairman.

◆ Do likewise with your parish councillors.

◆ When you are constructing your letters get your objection priorities right:

Example of a strong point – The local sewage system is already at overcapacity. Infrastructure renewal! Hellishly expensive to overcome! More than likely could scuttle the scheme.

Example of a weak point – A lovely view will be destroyed. So what! Needed houses are more important than weedy fields and a clump of old trees! Let's approve the scheme – it will clean up the landscape! No cutting edge so limited effect.

Cynical? Try it in your own campaign!

ACTION FOR CONSERVATION

This advice is for use in campaigns where the main issue is conservation.

◆ Contact all conservation groups locally and nationally for detailed advice. Try always to write to named people not faceless organisations. This requires good research but you cannot afford to 'buck the system', so make the effort – the campaign dividends justify it.

Contact important people locally and nationally, who are known to be involved in environmental issues.

◆ Study your own local environmental vulnerabilities. Search for vital ecological factors, e.g. unique or treasured local plant or animal species that could be endangered if their habitat is affected by the proposed development. As in marketing, identify your 'unique selling point' to promote your case.

An untrespassed ecosystem, sanctuary to fragile wildlife, will inevitably suffer damaging intrusion, when urbanisation is brought into the region. Where human beings concentrate, they explore and utilise the green zones within reach. If we were reliable and trustworthy guardians of the countryside, this would not be a criticism, but experience proves we are not. Butterflies, bats, frogs, newts, field flowers and certain ancient woodlands filled with bluebells, are now considered to be endangered if thoughtless urban expansion continues. Contact your local schools and enlist the teaching staff's help. The children are only too ready to research into such matters.

◆ Ask all interested groups to write formally and object to the proposed scheme.

◆ Write to your local M.P. and solicit his sympathies. Make this a vote issue. Make it a vote issue too with your local council representatives. You will soon find out how sensitive they are to threats of vote losses. We cannot overstress that politics is about keeping office. The threat of losing it, concentrates political minds in a remarkable way.

In summary: Be informed – Be relevant – Be concise and above all logical. If your style is blunt, dress it up with courtesy! Avoid pomposity and bombast. Remember, alienating people by arousing anger will guarantee failure for your cause.

SUMMARY OF CAMPAIGN ACTION AT PARISH LEVEL

◆ Plan for development revealed.

Request to have sight of plans at District Council Planning Offices. They cannot be borrowed or photocopied. Send someone discrete who can make a good sketch.

◆ Plans to hand (your sketch copies).

Assess impact on your local environment. Agree on unacceptablity.

Form action committee and decide on title.

◆ Compile action agenda.

Remember the 14 day rule for objecting. Conscript as many letter writers as possible.

Decide form and content of letters and write without delay to the members of the Parish Council.

◆ Six signatures needed to oblige the Parish Council to convene Parish Meeting.

If enough to hand among your committee members, draft letter to Parish Clerk forthwith. If not, search for sympathisers among uncommitted members of the community.

◆ Find a neutral venue, ahead of Parish Meeting, to rally other potential protesters – a church hall or any rentable public rooms. This may be among the expenses your members may have to subscribe to cover.

Canvas this meeting well. Since the main purpose of this meeting is to sort out the rationale of your campaign, avoid inadvertently inviting members of the Parish Council and possible known supporters of the proposals (there are bound to be some). They will be a possible source of contention.

The meeting should strive to be orderly. Insist on this. Even among friends passions can run high and could ruin the chances of rationalising purpose through disruptive discussion. Remember your purpose will be to gauge local sympathy and mobilise support for YOU, the objectors.

Feel satisfied that you have reached constructive aims and determined a practical plan of action.

◆ If support appears to be lacking:

Re-examine your original presentation and prepare for more aggressive door to door canvassing using your most persuasive members.

Advertise in your local press.

Seek editorial support among local publications.

SUMMARY OF ACTION CAMPAIGN AT DISTRICT LEVEL

◆ Deputise members to attend District Council meetings when they have your business on the agenda.

◆ Contact (in writing) local radio and television to bring your cause to a wider audience.

◆ Write protest letters to the local press.

◆ Write to your M.P. and environmental groups to gain support.

◆ Write to District Council planning officers and elected members sitting on the planning committee. Follow the protocol described earlier.

◆ Lobby individual members of the planning committee. Get to see them in person. Avoid getting into disputes – it will alienate them.

◆ Get as many people as possible to sign a petition to demand the District Council hold a site meeting before making a decision on the proposals.

6

WINNERS AND LOSERS

The Victorians used to say that man made the cities but God created the countryside.

'There is no countryside like the English countryside for those who have learned to love it.'

H. G. Wells wrote these sentiments in a beautifully descriptive eulogy on Britain published in 1910. In extolling a timeless truth, he endorsed a view that only the most purblind inhabitant of these islands would deny. Those of us who despair for what is left of his old vision, pause in sorrow to contemplate the tragedy of irreparable damage inflicted. Progress there must be but is the devastation we are all party to, necessary? One ponders the ugly legacy we are handing the future.

In our benign democracy there is agreement across the political spectrum that the freedom of the individual is 'holy writ'. Corporate and individual interests are accorded a freedom of action in pursuing their affairs bewildering to those of us who are obliged to witness and share the abuse they inflict on the hapless landscape.

No explanations or excuses could be admitted if it were not for the fact that everyone of us could be described as direct or indirect beneficiaries of what that abuse brings. Readers can use their own examples. We cite road building, housing and public utilities together with industries and business parks, all of which prefer to expand into easy greenfield sites.

In this country we tend to view environmental disasters in theoretical terms or on the drawing-board-of-possibility. We speak of radiation hazards inherent in the nuclear industries; in coal, of our smokestack contribution to acid rain and carbon dioxide emission. They are all much too fanciful for daily concern, even when we admit to their effect on global warming. As for the insidious loss of our fields and woodlands, it is too domestic a notion to deeply alarm us. This shrinking of concept and scale is unfortunate. The well-intentioned, but relatively powerless citizen, striving to make sense of all that passes for planning regulations and planning law, not to mention planning logic will be hard put to make intelligent reading of some of the narrative that follows.

Quite cynically, governments, developers and private individuals do collude to dump their unwanted schemes into the environment. Sometimes openly and sometimes by stealth or default they sidestep social obligations or fail to observe necessary standards of morality. Small wonder we experience difficulty in clinging to beliefs that natural justice and the sincerity of our fellow men are ever willing and ready to protect the greater interests of urban settlements and the countryside beyond.

'How can they allow it to happen?'

This question is often despairingly asked when inexplicable planning decisions challenge the credulity of helpless onlookers.

THE DISTRICT COUNCIL AS THE VILLAIN OF THE PIECE

We quote the case of the neighbouring village of Mateleigh. Their Parish Council threw out a scheme to redevelop the heart of this ancient village. The objections were dismissed when the scheme came before the District Council. The willingness of the Parish Council to compromise on a lower density development was ignored.

Impartial observers to the proceedings formed the view that the District Council welcomed 'outsider' developers. They seemed to go out of their way to give positive help and encouragement to their schemes, however unsuitable or damaging. Nothing seemed to deter this policy. Understandably the unfortunate communities being targetted became hotbeds of resentment.

Mateleigh was a case of proposed village expansion on a massive scale; to most people totally incomprehensible. As it was, the scheme united all local interests against its implementation. In the middle of the previous year, a non-statutory local plan had been adopted by the District Council; it was claimed after consultation with all the local resident community groups. Mateleigh Parish Council recognising the plan's conservation virtues, had asked for it to be made statutory so that it could be enforced by law. This was arbitrarily refused by the higher authorities.

However, the District Structure Plan which had already been adopted did contain development guides vaguely wrapped in words such as 'modest' and 'suitable'. The Mateleigh parish, appalled by what was being foisted upon them, appealed against the proposals and had the satisfaction of the Department of the Environment inspector's judgement. This stated that even the smaller scheme proposed by the Parish Council but rejected by the District Council would cause the Structure Plan to be exceeded by a large margin.

District Council chairman went so far at this stage to agree that the planning committee was bound by the Department of the Environment inspector's decision! It was also pointed out that the only people who were actively lobbying for the scheme were those who had interests in selling land to the developers. Furthermore, it was reliably reported that they had not been asked, as required by law, to declare their interest. Seemingly this reported-to-be state of affairs was passed off as 'unknown to the Chairman'.

The Parish Council's request to bring their intimate knowledge of local needs to the District Council planning meetings was refused! The wise appendices and amendments to the Department of Environment's own recommendations were thus denied the force of a public debate.

The game continued unfolding in the following fashion. Outline planning approval was agreed for the smaller scheme, which included some planning gains in the form of extra car parking facilities. The developers quickly came back for more and the subsequent scheme that was approved, more than doubled the number of proposed dwellings. An overkill result that, in effect, sealed the fate of charming rural Mateleigh, for in short the heart of the village would be destroyed.

The District Councillors had retreated in the face of the developer's threat to surcharge them individually with the costs of any appeal.

This threat was confirmed as legal by the District Council's solicitor. This alleged legality was later denied to the local M.P. but by this time matters had advanced too far to be reversed. The denial came in a reply from the Minister of the Environment to a Parliamentary question, seeking confirmation that failure to approve the unwanted scheme would involve the District Council in compensating the developers to the tune of £500,000 for loss of profits! The plaintiff's case would rest on unreasonable refusal.

A direct approach to the Secretary of State in the wake of this important denial, brought no satisfaction to the Parish Council. They were told that he could not intervene!

A great number of District Councils have acted timidly in the face of unacceptable planning applications, especially when confronted by powerful developers, in the belief that they could be accused of wilful misconduct, if it was seen that in their handling of the developer's application it was unjustly refused or watered down.

The last legal word on this matter suggested that this could not have been upheld in law given the prevailing circumstances. The Council had not lined themselves up behind local sentiments and needs. Had chosen to ignore all housing and commercial interests and finally CHICKENED OUT!

The narrative continued below sets out what must be seen as the sinister side of planning protocol. It will serve to enlighten the reader on 'behind the scenes' politics of local government.

THE POWER GAME ON THE VILLAGE GREEN – ANOTHER SIDE OF THE COIN!

Local and Parish Councils have no right of appeal against the big brother of higher planning authorities – county and ministry.

Parish Councils represent areas of differing sizes and complexities. They also have to deal with a great diversity of local matters. It is not to be wondered at, that they find themselves unable to cope with many cases presented to them when caught unawares and not primed by past precedents.

Higher planning authorities, although acknowledging that Parish Councils are often hard done by, still stick to the view that in all matters touching social and environmental concerns, they alone are the repositories of elevated vision, sounder technical knowledge and deeper wisdom, i.e. they know what is good for the people better than the people know what is good for themselves (c.f. Rousseau in the opening chapter)! Seemingly the rustics-down-on-the-green labour in darkness and never possess their biblical enlightenment. Small wonder these lesser mortals (us!) are dismissed, at their level, as fractious, contentious and totally lacking in the intellectual virtues vouchsafed to objective thinkers brooding in remote ivory towers of omnipotent judgement.

Furthermore, there appears to be no clear distinction in many voters' minds between legal powers and administrative practice. This casts questions on how these planning authorities reach their decisions, accepting or rejecting local recommendations. The apparent peremptory behaviour of higher bodies highlights the ill-defined and emasculated powers of Parish Councils. Few governing authorities will admit to this state of affairs – perhaps they dare not!

High-minded phrases such as: 'special difficulties', ' ... who has rights of appeal', 'questions of public interest' and 'unwarranted spending' are all raised as barriers to proper enquiry and due democratic process.

It appears that there is no legal obligations on the part of District Councils' planning departments to send Parish Councils detailed copies of planning applications. It hardly needs to be said that the parish in turn cannot comment sensibly on proposals without seeing plans in their wider context – not merely architects impressions or elevations.

LOCAL COUNCIL STATUS

The present powers of a parish or local council are set out in the Local Government Act 1972. Schedule 16; para 2 reads: 'Where a District Planning Authority have been notified in writing by the Council of the Parish ... that the Council wishes to be informed of every application for planning permission related to land in the Parish and to receive any such application, they shall inform the Parish Council in writing of the application.'

Beyond doing just that, the District Council have no further responsibility to spread enlightenment or to alert interested parties –

even if a perceived threat to local interests is noted! Certainly they have no obligation, in such circumstances, to let the Parish Council know.

NO PRIVILEGES ON THE GREEN

Since the Parish Council is not entitled to copies of the application or plans, it is not entitled to make recommendations. Nor, if any recommendations are made, does it oblige the planning authority to examine them. The only course of action left to the Parish Council is to take their turn with the public to go to the planning office and seek to inspect applications lodged at the District Council offices.

As these provisions do not resolve the status of the Parish Council, there seems little point in the tacit recognition in the provision by Parliament, that Parish Councils may wish to be involved in all planning applications at all stages. It must be said that in practice a better level of understanding and mutual goodwill does operate and few circumstances in local politics fail to be resolved harmoniously.

PRESUMPTION IN FAVOUR

The Department of the Environment Circular No. 14 issued July 1985 – paragraph 3 reads:

'There is always a presumption in favour of allowing applications for development having regard to all *material considerations*, unless that development would cause considerable harm to *interests* of acknowledged importance.'

'*Material*'. A consensus dictionary definition could read as – ' . . . a significant point likely to influence final decisions.'

'*Interests*' could be defined as:
1. Property interests in the area.
2. Advantage or detriment to visual amenity.

The authors interpret this as signalling the Department of the Environment's determination to be seen as fair and unobstructive in all planning matters, a view that is supported by what has been said earlier about development fulfilling local or national needs. Unfortunately for so much that lies at risk in our environments, the definition of material considerations introduces a disturbingly vague concept.

In the final analysis the planning authority decides if these requirements are met. We remind readers that planning authorities are not infallible. They can and do make mistakes; their mistakes can and do seriously damage the health of the countryside.

THE PHILOSOPHY OF THE FREE SPIRIT –

DOING YOUR OWN THING AND GETTING AWAY WITH IT

A planning application was filed by a multinational development group to develop an ancient and unspoilt area of meadowland in Gloucestershire. Alerted environmentalists recognised the unique character of the existing flora flourishing in the threatened area: a rich profusion of plants once so abundantly the glory of the English rural scene. The Society for the Protection of Rural England attempted to rush through a protection order and indeed one was prepared. However, a few hours before this could be served, the wiley developers, learning of the impending threat to their plans, sent in a squad of paid vandals who turned the area into a desert. After using herbicides to kill all vegetation, they completed the outrage by using heavy machinery to tear up the top soil.

Pictorial evidence showing the before and after situation could only have made sense to viewers convinced that they were witnessing the scene of a First World War battlefield! The commercial development subsequently went ahead doing what it had intended to do. The area is now part of a great urban housing sprawl linking town to town. Precedent and infilling has ensured that all brakes have been taken off the process of burying the regional countryside under tarmac and concrete.

A footnote to this catastrophic episode added the fact that the ruthless action on the part of the developers deprived a concerned conservation group of a proper chance to undertake 'a Noah's Ark rescue' of the rare wild flowers and other precious flora – not to mention whatever else flourished in that now vanished ecosystem.

IF SHEEP COULD FLY

An aggressive and clever West Country business tycoon was spoken of, by adversaries in his own planning district, with grudging admiration. This gentleman put in plans to improve his sheep farm. These were accorded the customary sympathy always given to farming interests. Approval was granted without comment. A few months later, the sheep farm had been transformed into an airfield with twelve acres of hangars and all the back-up buildings he cared to erect. To effect this transformation he had to lower the level of the site by nearly three meters, changing the whole configuration of the landscape in the process. The reader can imagine the scale of the development's impact by equating undulating fields and grazing sheep with the featureless flatness of an airfield runway, backed by the characterless appearance of the industrial-type service buildings. No challenge was offered by the local District Council planning officers. No enforcement notices were served. In the event the tycoon made no secret of the fact that abuse of planning law was an enjoyable pastime. He played to win and invariably did. He built unplanned roads, bridges and houses. He now enjoys an illustrious place in local legend as an invincible commercial James Bond! At the time of going to press he was still actively 'doing his own thing'. It must be said that he has the money to fight his way out of any legal difficulties, should his unapproved schemes encounter serious opposition. We return to this point later.

STEAM ROLLERING OPPOSITION

The national press have reported that a town bypass road is to be carved through a glorious stretch of the New Forest despite all local opposition, including that of the inspector of the Department of the Environment. It was said that the local district planners, determined to force the scheme through, raised enough money to get a private members bill through Parliament, scorning the local community charge payers who were powerless to act. The District Council planning spokesman allegedly dismissed their folly and shortsightedness in not having the prudence to capitulate before draconian action became necessary. The details, as reported, suggests there is plainly no morality in this kind of money! It must be said that there is no evidence that any of the funds, used to persuade Parliament, came out of the taxpayers' pockets. All this begs the question – can one buy the success of a Private Members Bill?

THE HORSE THAT BOLTED

A wealthy businessman, who was refused permission to build a house for his own occupation in a protected rural area got unopposed approval for a stable block. This type of development had the total sympathy of the rural pursuits lobby. Disregarding the terms and conditions attached to the approval he went on to build his intended dream home. No challenge was mounted by the local planners. They either ignored what was going on or condoned it. The house later went on the open market for £750,000.

The list of abuses is endless. The NIMBY has a hard and often thankless task in fighting ruthless and unscrupulous 'brass necks' who know only one law – their own. Grudgingly we are obliged to admire their boldness and deep knowledge of local planning laws – and all the loopholes. Their success in ignoring planning regulations does underline the importance of gaining such degrees of knowledge. After all, if by these means one can get round good laws, one can also defeat bad decisions using the same skills. It only serves to emphasise how much intelligent 'foot slogging' the unarmed citizen has to do. If this suggests we are in Wild West frontier days as far as planning is concerned we have to accept the fact! We add that what is at risk is not only the future but the present.

It must be stressed that the ordinary citizen who takes matters into his or her own hands and flaunts planning laws and regulations, rarely escapes the penalty of being served with an enforcement notice directing compliance with the contents of the order within twenty eight days. At the expiration of this time, punitive fines computed daily, are imposed. Theoretically this penalty is risked by all offenders, but once again we have to stress that this possibility is not viewed with the same apprehension if the transgressor has sufficient wealth to consider the risk worth taking.

WITH GREAT REGRET FARMER GILES CONCEDES THAT THE OAK STAIRWAY IN HIS NEWLY BUILT COWSHED IS PROVING IMPRACTICAL AND AFTER ONLY TWO DAYS HE MOVES HIS HERD ON

THE OFFER THAT DISTRICT PLANNING
DEPARTMENTS CANNOT REFUSE

A stratagem increasingly popular with large development groups seeking ways to get round apparently invincible local opposition to their mega-schemes, involves making planning gains that solve fundamental local needs available to intransigent councils.

Faced with what would appear to be a totally unyielding refusal, the developers shrewdly research local community infrastructure shortfalls, e.g. additional car parks, overcrowded roads requiring relief systems, lack of day-nursery facilities — this list is not exclusive. There is always something the community desperately wants but cannot afford. Cost conscious District Council planners these days fear to burden local people with massive capital programmes, as the sums involved are often calculated in millions of pounds. This factor will increase in importance since the introduction of the Community Charge.

The developers approach the matter in practical terms of project feasability. If what they want is profitable enough, the figure calculated to buy consent for the development (by adding the planning gain bait) merely becomes a premium easily affordable. The council is approached with an inclusive scheme and all considerations are turned on their heads as another precious bit of open country is sacrificed to the bulldozers.

Obviously the choice has to be weighed by the community affected. Who places a higher premium on environmental values or community gains, in these circumstances? It is also recognised that community gains can offer in some instances better value for land use. 'Unique environmental factors' must always determine how the decision turns.

Knowledgeable readers may dismiss this simplistic view of the game-of-planning-gain. We accept their charge without retracting the principle of the matter.

7

PLAN TO GO TO APPEAL – A PLANNING EXPERT'S NOTES

The appeals department of the D.O.E. is viewed by some, with justification on occasions, as the developer's friend. Freed from the constraints of local politics and politicians, many people are fearful that an inspector will be unaware of local concerns and view the planning application with a panoramic objectivity, listening only to the unemotive, practical arguments of the developer:

'Our proposals will preserve and enhance the very best that the local environment has to offer ...'

'Demand for housing will not simply go away if this site is not developed ...'

'The locality will miss out on a unique opportunity ...'

'The planning gain is enormous ...'

There is, and always will be, something very seductive in the hyped images developers conjure up around well-planned schemes packed with vital urban amenities.

In addition, there is always the remarkable view taken, that development of a particular unspoilt open space or rural region, will somehow 'open it up for all to enjoy'. The inference being that those opposing the scheme wish selfishly to hold onto a unique amenity that should be freely available to everyone. The fact that such development invariably buries whatever delights the eye under thousands of tons of concrete, entombing whatever it had going for it more permanently than an archaeological ruin, thus denying everyone a chance to enjoy what was the previously unspoilt, makes the argument both morally and practically unsustainable.

It is well worth noting that the appeal procedure is not solely used as the place of last resort after all other means of persuasion have failed. Some developers take their applications straight to the D.O.E., ignoring local channels on the grounds that their case will only be delayed if they go through the local committee process. Others will file plans with both the local authority and the D.O.E. This process is known as 'dual tracking' and serves to remind the local planners that should matters be delayed or deferred for any length of time, they will remove the locally lodged plans and initiate an appeal straight to the D.O.E. Some developers, namely the more unscrupulous, will lodge one plan at local level and a slightly different one with the D. O.E. If the two plans differ on proposed density of development, e.g. if local plans show six houses per acre and D.O.E plans show fifteen per acre, the plans lodged at local level — no matter how unacceptable they are in principle — may well prove to be the lesser of the two evils. Such dilemmas created for the local planning department may cause them to be accused of acting unreasonably if they are not prepared to view the application before them in a spirit of compromise. If the result was for the District Council to refuse the entire scheme, the strength of regional precedent becomes the paramount deciding factor. For example account would be taken of the existing surrounding development and whether the proposed development falls within the area housing framework. This may well be sufficient to allow the higher density to go through on appeal.

Two very important points should be noted from these given examples. Firstly, a plan that follows a course through the local committee system and is handled by local authority planning officers, allows for a higher degree of control through negotiations between the developers and the officers. Frequently a decision made on appeal ties the officers' hands, denying them the right to negotiate on a specifically, less imposing type of dwelling. The community may for example get houses when it would have preferred bungalows! The D.O.E. inspector, in his ivory tower and in his wisdom, could decide that four-bedroomed houses was the proper answer to local housing needs, notwithstanding the fact that everyone else wanted single-storey residences! Obviously the critical point here is to guard against this possible danger.

SUMMARY: Application in for bungalows — refused at local level because no housing is acceptable to local planning intentions.

Matter goes to appeal — D.O.E. likes the idea of the development and furthermore decides two-storey houses answers housing needs more realistically than bungalows!

So we see a refusal of a given application for development greeted with a great sense of relief. One hardly needs to dwell on the depth of local dismay when events prove the exact opposite.

ADVICE: Listen to the arguments advanced by the officers. If they are convinced that their formula for conducting the case is right, given all the prevailing local circumstances, and, if you can identify your interests with their view of the chances of a fair outcome on appeal, even if you have to compromise, go along with them. If the arguments are firmly stacked against you, winning at local level will only be a pyrrhic victory.

Bear in mind that under the dictum of the 1947 Town and Country Planning Act, no planning permission should be 'unreasonably withheld'. Refusals should be based on evidence that shows that the granting of consent will lead to 'demonstrable harm'.

'Beauty is in the eye of the beholder'. A universal truth!

By the same token ' Ugliness is in the eye of the beholder'.

A cynical but reasonable contention. One could also add that whatever is environmentally ugly is often to business minds, commercially beautiful — if it comes cheaply! We suspect that few developers would deny this to be true.

The reader is invited to pass judgement on the aesthetic qualities of D.I.Y. superstores mushrooming in sensitive urban areas. Try viewing them dispassionately against the charm of Victorian or Edwardian terraces. Look at their impact on any urban environment that boast buildings inherited from our more gracious built-of-bricks past.

PUBLIC INQUIRY

When there is clash between what the developer believes to be 'unreasonably withheld consent' and what the local authority believes to be the factor of 'demonstrable harm' in the application, an appeal procedure is set in motion.

If the inspector from the Department of the Environment deems the case to be of significant public interest, he will call a public inquiry. At such an inquiry the inspector will listen to both sides of the argument and equally important, will note all written evidence from the public, either for or against the application. The inspector may well call upon an appointed spokesperson to state both sides of the citizens' case, especially if there is enough local opposition.

Where and when there is great public concern, a number of steps should be taken in order to register that concern and achieve the maximum impact.

THE APPEAL

Some of this advice duplicates, in substance, matters that have been touched on when discussing the handling of disputes at local level. However, it is worth a second mention. To begin with, a notification of the date of appeal will be sent to the local authority, so make sure you are aware of the date. Your district and parish councillors will have the details. You will have precisely twenty-one days from the date of the letter in which to mount a letter-writing-campaign and send the details to the Department of the Environment.

◆ Do not make the mistake of addressing correspondence to the local council or councillors generally — you are simply wasting time and the letters may never reach their proper destination. Write to named people.

◆ Make certain that on the date of the public inquiry as many people as possible turn up. The officers representing your interests, fighting on your behalf, will be greatly encouraged by enthusiastic attendance, clearly underlining local concern and support. This will emphasise the strength of local feeling to the inspector.

◆ As we have already said, at the opening of the inquiry the inspector's policy in all cases is to call on those attending to present arguments for and against the application. It is wise to make certain that whoever speaks, does so effectively, above all addressing every point in a relevant fashion. Furthermore he or she should support the line adopted by the planning officers in a clear-cut presentation.

◆ Avoid any tendency to wander off the point. Make time privately in the run-up to the occasion to rehearse your points if you are unused to addressing public audiences. This also affords time to sort out, in your own minds, the strong arguments from the weak. Nothing is more demoralising than finding the effort to emphasise your case, causing your line of thought to become confused.

◆ Whatever happens, do not commit the folly of heaping emotive verbage on the appellant, all of which will be totally disregarded by the inspector. The net result will be to weaken your case and possibly undermine the effort of your planning officers. Guard against this!

Obviously no-one can determine the outcome of an appeal, other than the inspector. However, win or lose, at least you should feel at the end of your presentation that the justice of your case has been fully and cogently argued. The manner of your presentation, your tact and your logic will determine this and should ensure it.

NEGOTIATING TO OBTAIN BETTER RESULTS IN A LOST CAUSE

The applicant wins his case — the battle is lost!!

NOT ENTIRELY TRUE! Development there will be, but a vital battle over details has just begun!

Planning applications are usually made in two stages: outline planning permission and then detailed planning permission. It is unlikely that the applicant will file for detailed planning permission in one go. Therefore only the principle for the development, in the form of 'outline consent', will be approved first. You now have the opportunity to fight the developer when he puts in his detailed plans.

This in itself can mean a long and protracted process of negotiations, with plans being submitted only to be amended and then resubmitted. On each occasion, the process of consultation will have to take its course and on each occasion the upmost vigilance must be maintained. Indeed the lobbying process can even be stepped up. Remember you are no longer fighting to prevent the development, the principle has been established. Time and energy will be wasted if an emotional backlash is allowed to dominate your plans to fight a campaign of damage limitation. It is possible to win major concessions throughout the planning procedure as conditions and agreements are attached to the final application. For example, house type, i.e. bungalow or chalet bungalow may be applicable if larger properties would seriously affect local urban balance and obliterate views — although the loss of a view is, unfortunately, not a planning consideration in itself. Landscaping and a tree planting/retention scheme will have to be submitted to the satisfaction of the local authority.

Make certain that tree preservation orders (T.P.O.) are in place and that no development will take place until the proposals for landscaping are satisfactory.

Acting retrospectively on these matters is very difficult and conditions are almost impossible to reverse once development is under way. Think ahead.

*Example:*If bungalows only are to be built on part or all of the site — in order to preserve housing balance and not intrude into views — make certain that 'permitted development rights' are withdrawn. If they are not, then the house owner can quite easily apply to extend the dwelling and create an additional room in the roof, thus converting the bungalow into a chalet bungalow.

THE NEW LANGUAGE OF PLANNING

Local planning authorities are now extending their conceptual vocabulary in order to create terms that define in mentally visual ways the acceptable face of development. Terms such as:

◆ *Roofscape.* It is a dominant feature of towns and villages. It is often of greater interest when viewed from above, but from any angle, roofscape gives character and identity to a town, village or any group of well-designed buildings. However, it is especially important in localities of domestic urbanisation. No individual, who has travelled widely, can fail to have been enchanted by the picturesque, variegated roofscapes of old towns and villages scattered across the length and breadth of Europe, (not excluding Britain where the fabric of older communities has survived). No-one sensitive to the charm and beauty of such structural additions to a particular land-scape would argue that they are anything other than visually enhanc-ing.

◆ *Skyline.*This should not be confused with roofscape. It is vital in both urban and rural environments; in particular, when placing new buildings in an established landscape, the skyline – taking account of silhouettes of existing buildings and local topography – must be respected. This applies especially where the environment is encompassed by hill ridges or any other naturally occurring feature of the region that might be properly described as its 'frame'.

◆ *Topography.*It is the natural or artificial features of a land-scape, town or urban district.

◆ *Aspect – Prospect – Orientation.*This recognises the need to avoid regimented developments by harmonising all buildings with the contours of the landscape. To achieve an aesthetically successful result, a detailed survey of the site in its widest aspect must precede development.

Further, aspect and orientation are concerned with the positioning of a development in relation to the position of the sun in order to gain maximum advantage of sunlight playing on northern or southern aspects of the site.

◆ *Cluster Houses and Terraces.*Properly planned clusters of houses give protection from wind and rain, are energy saving and afford economy of land use.

◆ *Access.*Compacting housing development allows the possi-bility of achieving good access without excessive road length.

◆ *Site stability.*This depends on the subsoil and obviously the wider issues of land survey come into discussion and planning.

The above terms are being used interpretatively and increasingly across the country to isolate the qualities in landscape or townscape unique to regions, in order to arrive at qualities of design and place-ment that will enhance the locality designated for development. It is an attempt to give planners and developers a code of good manners that will avoid creating 'blots on the landscape'. It leans heavily on the existing order of things and in many ways, especially since Prince Charles has become a leading advocate of such concerns, pays a great

Frequently, a developer may choose to ignore all of the above in addition to flaunting planning terms and conditions. If tree roots are severed and hedgerows grubbed, additional plots may well be created. It is therefore essential that during development every stage is observed to ensure that this does not happen. Where it does and the developer has broken a planning agreement, the enforcement officer should be informed. The intention should clearly be to put right the wrong that has been committed. The policy adopted towards transgressions must be tough. Citizens should not be timid about informing against the unscrupulous. In the case of the lost tree or hedge it is essential that the developer is made to replant immediately.

It should be noted, of course, that one way of securing additional protection for trees is to make certain that they are visibly fenced in. This should overcome the argument, often resorted to by way of excusing developers' vandalism, that it is impossible to inform every member of their staff as to which tree has, or has not, got a preservation order (T.P.O.) placed on it. An obvious fence will overcome this often cited and speciously used ploy.

Readers are advised to go-to-it. Your environment will only get the protection you give it. The way a development turns out must reflect the degree to which you have galvanised yourself and your neighbours in its proper and responsible implementation. Failure to rescue your patch of Britain , when it is possible, from desecration by those that are determined to break the rules, merely underlines your own lack of interest in your home location and your apathy towards what goes on around you.

8

PROTESTERS WITHOUT A CAUSE

'People who value their own backyards
should not kick down their neighbours' fences.'
NIMBY PROVERB

Man, the social animal has been in the business of protesting since
two and two made up a tribe. We all harbour privately perceived
views of our personal and social needs and regard such matters as
protected by singular, inalienable, democratic rights. In public or in
private, when these rights are thought to be at risk, abused or
trampled on, most of us react by protesting. Our tolerance thresholds
and flashpoints are, of course, uniquely ours and all visible responses
in such circumstances are regarded by outsiders from their equally
personal and valid view of what is reasonable to themselves. If
privately each of us remains happily a mystery to the rest of the
world, in public we are naked. When we overreact to events in which
we are involved, whatever our inner views of the provocation, judged
by detached or critical opinion our behaviour may be condemned as
indefensible. To gain sympathy for one's cause, responses must not
offend the sensitivities and sensibilities of others. If they do, the
person, not the cause becomes the issue.

These are increasingly politicised days and the right to protest has
become enshrined in our moral social charter. It offers a way of life to
many individuals and groups. Entrenched in their personal Bill of

Rights, such groups only appear to thrive when actively engaged in confronting the bogy establishment.

Few of us need reminding that pressure and ginger groups are as thick on the ground as houses. And it must be said, society is in general healthier for it. To extend the narrative into this intriguing area of enquiry would be a highly diverting but unproductive trespass, outside the remit of our original brief. However, the phenomenon of protest highlights some aspects of 'protest protocol' worthy of discussion.

We said in an earlier passage 'know what you are protesting about'. The exercise is a leap in the dark, so try to give some thought as to where you might be landing. Two short accounts given below point salutary lessons. They are taken from real situations and only slightly coloured by the authors' explanatory observations.

SOMETHING FISHY

A farmer, doubtlessly rationalising his commercial viability, placed on the market a pair of picturesque stone barns with the benefit of approval for converting into domestic dwellings. The view from the rear of the properties, across open rolling countryside, was, in the words of one of the people involved in the event, 'wonderful'. For most of us, it could be said 'a living dream realised'. The barns were not long selling (to two different purchasers) and hardly longer in being attractively refurbished. The proud new owners moved in.

One family loved and kept dogs, a potent source of latent friction with most farmers. They tend to view with suspicion any dogs not their own. Understandable when one considers the widespread havoc caused by unsupervised pets worrying livestock, especially sheep. Country news and gossip is full of reported cases of dogs straying onto fenced farmland to savage valuable farm animals. Obviously neither side had considered dog ownership as a contentious issue when the sale of the barns was being negotiated. Nor did it surface as a problem in the early days of neighbourliness. In the event, it seemed the dogs in question were well behaved and controlled.

Family number two did not keep animals and appeared to have taken up residence quietly. The auguries were good for settled relationships between the farmer and his new neighbours.

One day the inevitable doggy trespass occurred – without serious consequences. Words were exchanged between the farmer and the dog owners but the event seemed to pass off quietly enough. However, as is often the way in such apparently insignificant incidents, the dog owners thought the farmer had exceeded his authority. It left them with a sense of grievance.

Some time after this episode, rumour, shortly to prove fact, revealed the farmer had intentions to develop part of his land as a fish farm, breeding and rearing trout and allowing use for anglers.

The 'fish farm disclosure' provoked widespread hostility in the local village and protest meetings were held in the village hall. A campaign committee was formed.

The key objection centred on common fears of:

◆ Disturbed status quo.

◆ Intensified use.

◆ Increased traffic.

◆ Noise pollution.

In short all the reasonable apprehensions felt by communities confronted with changes happening in their midst.

The new residents directly overlooking the development site became high-profile protesters. They were duly marked as such by the farmer. Shrewdly he held his peace until he had successfully gained approval for his proposals.

At this point comment must be made that of all possible scenarios available to the farmer, installing a trout farm was certainly as environmentally friendly as is conceivable. No large intrusive structures were proposed. It could be argued, probably was, that by placing fish ponds in the foreground of the landscape an enhancement factor was being added to the view. It has been well said that 'a view over water is as therapeutic as a tranquilliser'. Certainly the meditative preoccupations of anglers denied credibility to those insisting that their presence could damage the settled rural peace by encouraging unacceptable activities that incite unsociable noise. Anglers are not known to indulge in 'lager-lout antics' even when they land outsized fish.

As the ponds' construction got under way, the new residents were disconcerted to find the farmer using the excavated spoil to construct a high earthwork directly obstructing their lovely view. This traditional rural bank infringed no planning regulations. Indeed such structures are welcome wherever they can be raised in preference to less environmentally sympathetic forms of fencing. In line with farming practices such banks are heightened by planting the crest with beech or blackthorn thickets. The total height achieved in known examples attaining three meters, provided the hedges are kept well trimmed.

Further protests in this case proved to be of no avail. The farmer was exercising his proper right to fence his land appropriately. Furthermore he was performing a social service by screening from his neighbours, most emphatically, the activities they had themselves imagined to be a potentially damaging nuisance. He could quote, in his defence, the testimony of many protest meetings called to block his reasonable scheme.

The fact that he had deprived them of a fine view was of no concern to him or the planning authority. Although he had sold them the barns, he had not sold them a view! At the heart of the matter was the loss of goodwill − the first casualty of unreasonableness. We stress this, as it is perhaps the most precious component of conciliation available in situations of conflict. Always study and appreciate what is really involved and adapt your thinking to the wider implications of the situation. The farmer wanted to continue a rural use. He was not seeking approval for a factory!

STORM IN A MILLPOND

The second story concerns a garden and a derelict water mill.

A husband and wife motivated by purposes as laudable as can be imagined, acquired a neglected parcel of land on which stood a decaying, ancient mill. This was within an area of outstanding natural beauty. After overcoming many difficulties, including planning disputes with district planning committees, they fashioned about the restored mill a garden described by a leading regional garden authority as one of the loveliest springtime gardens in the country.

The owners duly obtained whatever blessing they needed from the local authority and opened the gardens to the public. They registered as a charity to ensure there were no 'profit motives'. It was a move that denied the possibility of the project being promoted as a commercial tourist attraction.

75

Fighting the Developers

Notwithstanding the visible proof of their worthy intentions, they became the victims of an invidious campaign of denigration, carried on in the letter columns of the local press. The writer's (a single voice) undoubted intention was to arouse hostility and prevent public patronage of the garden. No-one could doubt his sour determination to undermine the scheme and secure its closure.

His arguments were predictable and stale: damage done to existing, environmentally precious, structures (ancient banks and hedges); encroachment on unspoilt land with bricks and concrete; thousands of extra visitors bringing cars and coaches; vast advertising campaigns, putting rural remoteness and tranquillity under threat! Thrown in for good measure was a sinister claim that it was all a hypocritical ploy to cash in on the project, at a convenient moment, and make off with 'speculators' profit'.

Despite the 'single voice' element, intense and widespread public concern was stirred up. There was plenty of proof that the environment, far from being threatened, was being reinstated and properly managed. Much public time was taken up examining the complaints, but the planning authorities eventually took the view that only dedicated garden lovers would find it rewarding to visit. It was no Disneyland. Due in part to a tolerant regional press, the campaign rumbled on for over a year, happily getting nowhere. But one is forced to examine the psychology of individuals driven obsessively to voice unjustified and fixated ideas. There were certainly no matters of communal interest at stake to justify this spiteful attempt to abort a scheme whose purpose, however deeply investigated, could only be proved enhancing both to the community and the environment. Beware therefore of using unsubstantiated fears or reasons when protesting. Beware, when indulging in personal grudges, of risking disclosing motives that might reveal disturbed personality traits, perhaps opening, in the public domain, serious challenges to one's own integrity or state of mind.

It seems appropriate at this point to leave the reader with this observation by the great seventeenth century writer and thinker, Daniel Defoe.

> 'Nature has left this tincture in the blood
> That all men would be tyrants if they could.'

9

PAST, PRESENT AND FUTURE

A REFLECTION

The world is changing; has there ever been a time when this truth has not impressed itself, often painfully, on the consciousness of human-kind? Yet in the pastoral milieu of former days, certainly up to the age of the Industrial Revolution, society did have historic space in which to pause and reflect. It might be said, with justification, mis-takes could always be rectified. Environmental damage, whether inflicted by man or nature, was mercifully restored – in time.

Nature healed while man stood by, passively awaiting the conso-lation of the seasons of God.

Even the Industrial Revolution built with human scale in mind. Were those dark mills really so satanic?

What remains to us of that recently condemned past we rush to list and to preserve. Time gives us space and perspective to re-appraise and even applaud the architectural good manners of the nineteenth century industrial planners. The satanic element refers to the back-wardness of that period's legislature; perfectly excusable if we are all prepared to accept that every epoch is a prisoner of its own time. If current enlightened trade union practices, together with the benefits of modern medicine and hygiene had applied in those days we would, no doubt, find good cause to add that era's working conditions to our list of golden nostalgias. It is also true that centres of industry were clearly defined islands of smoke and sweat beyond which, within walking distance, stretched endless rich rural acres. This renewable seasonal joy was available for all who moved the machinery of industry and commerce. It was also sanctuary to countless species of now vanished wildlife. Those habitats then still seemed as secure as they had been since the dawn of time. We recall the memorable image in the novel *How Green is My Valley*, of the miner, who knew that when he touched the roof of the coal seam he was working, he could feel the fields where the corn was green!

Again, who would deny that the cosy rows of Victorian back-to-back houses, lacking only decent sanitation and efficient heating offered welcomingly superior domestic opportunities to the family, in stark contrast to the often inhuman packaging of contemporary designer estates and tower-blocks. Victorian houses, which survive, we cherish, modernise and inhabit with pride. The latter we are beginning to remodel, cut down or in other ways modify and often where this refurbishment is not possible, we rid ourselves of their presence by blowing them up!

To all past urbanisations, whether they owe their existence to good government or bad, we must add the indisputable fact that they stayed or were swept away but were rarely succeeded by something worse. What is more, it can be claimed that the environment survived! In the main, building styles and manners changed, but concepts of civic beauty and the rightness of mans' work within the civic confines were governed by the prevailing constraints of communal pride and consensus good taste. One could intrude into the existing order of things, however idiosyncratically, provided one exerted proper concern and judgement. Dickensian Britain might be cited to deny this truth, but by Charles Dickens's time the black side of the industrial revolution was emptying the countryside in its hunger for labour and had not produced the social enlightenment needed to overcome the challenges thrown up by the speed of urban change.

RICH LEGACIES AND CONTEMPORARY BLUNDERS

Fitting 'breathing spaces' into urban areas is one excellent example of our predecessors' proper concern for the needs of the civic soul. City parks, squares, gardens and open spaces are not the products of twentieth century planning enlightenment. We have inherited them from far-sighted forbears who 'thought green' and planted for a future they knew they would not live to see. They did not know a world in crisis but they did understand the works of their Creator enshrined in the natural order of things: the hopeful cycles of growth and decay. Men learned to respect, value and use the seasons wisely as they took stock of the green legacies of the years. The controversial architectural language of twentieth century planners, introduced by the late Le Courbusier, who once described houses and cities as machines for living in, would have been incomprehensible to the urban visionaries of former days. His planning ideology has taken such a hold on our contemporary thinking that it has become a planning mandate for our entire way of life. Armed with such sterile portfolios, is it to be wondered at that town and country planners, wedded to expedience and speculative interests, shed their sentiments and sensibilities in an often brutal disregard for human needs and man's spiritual values?

Historians are fond of attaching to epochs, terms designed to encapsulate the main cultural thrust of their societies. We recognise the seventeenth and eighteenth centuries as the ages of reason and enlightenment; how would we describe our present age? Speed in all things: travel, communication, fast food, crisis management. All these have undermined our values and imparted to our collective psyche the 'gene' of instant gratification. Instant disposability too! Will history judge our consumer society, with its inbuilt obsolescence and creeping pollution, as the 'Age of Destruction'? We all long for life certainties, that in turn creates some notion of human permanence .It is a fundamental yearning, without which all our higher expectations become destabilised. Manipulate time as we will, human past, present and future collide in painful confusion, made all the less palatable by the logic of contemporary technology. Computer predictions leave us with few illusions about what lies in store for the world.

Society's catch phrase is: 'Why wait?'

Given the individual's concern with selfish objectives – no bad thing if the earth's bounty was inexaustible – we are currently being forced to come to terms with our earlier premise, namely the planet's finite resources. These are assets that are being sucked dry by man's insatiable needs and aspirations.

RESTATING THE CASE

We started this book with a planning conflict over a green valley that was to be sacrificed to provide family homes. It might well have been lost to an urgently needed hospital or school or shopping precinct; or an industrial estate, seen as vital in providing much needed employment. The moral dilemmas confronting today's society are profound and dig uncomfortably into our awareness. Small wonder they torment our responses. We have many choices but few options. The planet's survival chances are boxing mankind into an inescapable corner.

We find all arguments come back to the fundamental and indisputable fact — the individual can eat, drink, smoke and otherwise abuse himself to death; it is his or her private affair! However, no society can claim to be civilised and responsible if it does not decently house and employ its people.

Democracies must find their own answers. We do not need brave-new-world philosophies to regiment us into scientifically measured, regulated and controlled lives. The great issues concerning planet management are likely to create draconian political traps, apart from involving our best scientific brains well into the next millenium . It hardly needs to be stressed that only man's capacity to make use of his intelligence, rather than muscle, will decide whether we turn earth into heaven or hell. At regional, domestic level we can make a small start by agreeing that one great need is the proper and appropriate recycling of available land and resources. Great tracts of disused land are historically and conveniently situated within existing urbanised areas. It cannot be argued that derelict sites are not to be had in plenty. Currently, statistics show only 50% of land available for reclamation is recycled for domestic building. Much of this land is located where it is most needed. Think how its imaginative use would lift the outlook and morale of our people. Such initiative requires morality and responsible freewill to co-exist in intelligent partnership.

Any attempt to satisfy the nation's housing needs by a reckless assault on our green acres must be resisted wherever it is reasonable and right so to do. Man's last great crusade is being launched to defend the Earth. Urban man must help the greater movement by gathering his forces to defend our shrinking regions of natural beauty.

The well-publicised threat to the Earth's protective atmosphere is creating high-level panic, but at our feet, in water and on dry land, a precious universe of animal and plant life continues to pass into oblivion, driven there by insensitivity and thoughtlessness. We have long known the truth of this Dodo Syndrome – once species are lost, whether they be elephants or insects, they are gone for ever. We cannot afford to lose a single living creature from this earth! Man either wakes up to this self evident truth or he joins the other lost species in oblivion!

Human beings live to accept the inevitability of death but take comfort from the fact that the earth is part of an eternity, promising immortality. Man, in the face of, and despite this sublime gift, is threatening to destroy his one and only habitat. Individually we must ask ourselves – can we afford to be part of the killing pack?

'Saving is a greater art than gaining.'

Old German proverb

TYING THE ENDS

Since Nicholas Ridley quit the Department of the Environment, it has been alleged that a wind of change is blowing through its corridors, creating new thinking with greater emphasis on a sympathetic approach to Britain's environment. Housing policies are rightly aimed at meeting the need to provide new homes. We are soothed with a tacit assurance that their provision will be reconciled to environmental protection policies, in both town and country.

Previously, economic development and economic growth were overriding factors. Now the need to reconcile such provisions with conservation and enhancement, is on the agenda. Among the many recommendations is that the character of villages should always be respected, both in regard to the density of their populations and rural setting. Perhaps we can hope that this new thinking will herald the end of urban blight – an end to high- rise-obsessions and a return to human scale and beauty in city redevelopment and refurbishment, making them places where people want to be.

However, the current guidelines concerning building designs is disappointing. Beyond asking developers to aim for high quality designs, together with sympathetic landscaping, it leaves details very much in their hands. Furthermore it paradoxically states that it is rarely justified to impose controls over design details. This is fine, if you trust all the people involved. Since good design is the essence of a total concept, bad detailing can and will destroy any scheme. So again we see the intention to upgrade the demands of good planning and design is being jeopardised by a loose and indecisive approach to overall regulating. If departmental advice is not enough to instill good manners, compulsion should be introduced, with adequate provision to spread the net and ensure compliance. How depressing to have to conclude that, left to their own devices, human beings are incapable of cultivating good taste or conserving for its own sake. Every planning department should be made to answer one question when dealing with new applications for any type of building – 'Would our officers or elected members agree to either live in it, or coexist with it, if the choice had to be made?' If the answer is no, then the project should be consigned to the waste bin!

Notwithstanding the improved thrust of the Department of the Environment's policies, it would appear inevitable that large tracts of virgin countryside will continue to vanish under the tracks of earth-movers and bulldozers. Events detailed below confirm these fears. We add, with dismay, the most recent entry to the debate.

ANOTHER PITCH

Prince Charles was recently quoted as saying:

'Cornwall needs development but not at any price.'

This comment opened up discussion in January 1990 on a series of bad planning decisions that have been promulgated in the county. However widespread the concern for good planning and however much public alarm increases and however urgent the imperative to protect the countryside becomes, men of power in local government continue to go their own perverse ways. We stand by helplessly as more irreplaceable rural acres vanish under concrete. What emerges from various reports also suggests that a great number of the successful building applications were the result of insider lobbying and clubroom camaraderie. The examples given below show elected members blatently overturning the recommendations of the professional planning officers on countless occasions. We add the admitted fact that the applications, in question, broke planning guidelines and regulations in almost every case.

◆ Three instances disclosed planning approval to build bungalows on Council owned land. Approval was given, on medical grounds, to retiring Council members. The same department refused a disabled war veteran's application to construct a bungalow, for his own occupation, on a similar privately owned site! Clearly democracy and oligarchy maintain an uneasy alliance in these corridors of power, especially when fair dealing and natural justice are openly disregarded along with private contempt for public probity. One vice chairman resigned in protest over the planning policies of his fellow councillors. It is only fair to add that Whitehall too had issued warnings to this body, but was ignored.

Cornwall's county planning committee came to the bleak conclusion that most district councils are riding roughshod over national and local attempts to save landscapes from despoilation by unnecessary building.

◆ Under another heading, disclosure was made that the Local Government Ombudsman had castigated the North Cornwall District Council for maladministration, after it granted permission to a couple to build a second home hot on the heels of completing their first! We quote various comments:

'The committee [of elected members] has granted personal planning permissions on so many occasions that it would have been difficult for the planning officer or the council's solicitor to have advised members what they were about to do was wrong.'

'Clearly the council should mend its ways.'

In their defence of elected members, senior council officers denied the suggestion that the decisions were corrupt.

'We do not believe that money has changed hands.'

The fact that the notion was mooted at all, makes the matter an appalling case for outsiders to reconcile.

'Inconsistent planning decisions create fears of corruption we agree, but these are humane decisions! Members hear of an old man with sciatica and say why shouldn't he have a bungalow on his own land?'

Yes — Maybe! Nevertheless, we return to the inconsistencies highlighted above and again point to the awkward questions they raise.

◆ Furthermore one county planning chief suggested that guidelines were ignored in at least 200 instances in 1988, on sites recommended for special protection.

With more people leaving farming and less land wanted for growing the food we need (the authors ask — is there not alleged to be a world food shortage?) there is pressure throughout the whole of Britain, on all planning departments to relax controls in formerly protected regions. Still the question remains:

'How can the public trust decisions made on their behalf, when within a short time of buying into a protected area beside a green belt, new building sites, more often than not breaching regulations, thrust into the landscape?'

District planners are entrusted to protect the interests of rural Britain — both current and future. They should be put on notice to do just that, or give way to more responsible local government.

Man's greatest achievements began as acts of faith. Today the need for faith in humankind's future has never been greater.

COURAGE OF CONVICTIONS

Individuals will always doubt their own ability to influence great social issues. The question all thinking members of society so often ask themselves is — what is going wrong around us and what can be done to change things for the better? Finding answers to this dilemma becomes increasingly relevant when planet catastrophes are being witnessed and debated. Do not despair. If the world is going to be saved at all, it will be rescued by countless small acts of thoughtful responsibility undertaken by dedicated and devoted citizens, willing to become front-line fighters in defence of their small patch of green earth. The first step is to recognise the urgency. The second is to believe in the action one proposes to take and lastly to believe in oneself. Then muster the determination and resolve to be positive and carry on, despite the strength of the forces opposing your chosen cause.

In making this last statement, we remind readers we are not, in the activists' sense, a political voice and our concerns cover action against environmental spoilation that can be undertaken intelligently within the framework of this country's laws.

Saving a field of wild flowers in Berkshire from the bulldozers, may seem a far cry from the horrendous destruction of the rain forests of Brazil. Believe us it is not.

Future generations of earth survivors will thank the far sighted ordinary people of Britain who cared, every bit as much as they will great leaders, who one day will finally agree among themselves to rationalise and mobilise man's collective efforts in defence of the Earth. The qualities needed are enthusiasm, determination and tenacity.

To all of you out there who care, we say — stay with it and good luck!

PEOPLES' SONG

Hitler was right.
Stalin was right.
Revolution was right.
Anarchy was right.
Democracy was right.
Totalitarianism was right.
Genocide was right.
Hiroshima was right.
Christianity was right.
Judaism was right.
Islam was right.
Destruction was right.
Persecution was right.
Pollution was right.
Famine was right.
Prejudice, brutality, barbarism, revenge, hate, murder,
War . . . all of them right.
Man was right.
Man was right.
Man was right.
Man was right.
Man was right.
Man was right.

Collected Poems 1944 – 1990. Gerald Moore.

This poetic paradox is included as an ironic comment on the contradictions inherent in human thinking and behaviour. We do not underestimate the enormity of the task facing those that would strive to create a secure and stable world. Unfortunately the values that could ensure the planet's survival do not yet govern the hearts and minds of men. Until we speak a common language that expresses a love for the Earth and all creatures that dwell on it, the threat of extinction will grow.

Living is a series of tiny acts of faith strung together during each human lifetime as a means of coming to terms with an incomprehensible state, man calls existence.

Bless the endeavours of all those who share our sentiments.

APPENDIX 1

ARCHEOLOGY – TREASURES UNDER THREAT

As we respond to the demands of today's society to reconstruct and refurbish towns and villages in line with contemporary needs, we steadily destroy one of our most precious cultural assets – our past. During the last eighty years at least 50% of all known archeological sites have been lost. If we include in this tally artifacts above ground – embracing ancient buildings whose adaptation have served mans' needs for countless generations, the losses must be seen as appalling.

Nothing condemns man's time on Earth more than poverty of spirit and failure of intellect. Nevertheless, the planning bureaucrat and entrepreneur, busy designing schemes to build shopping malls in the oldest quarter of town, or business parks on Saxon settlements, ensure that it is happening all the time. To be fair to those involved, an awareness among developers is leading to a wider concern and certainly more and more chances are being given to knowledgeable organisations to mount rescue digs before precious sites vanish under concrete. We agree that ancient sites yield little in the way of satisfaction to the vast number of people disinterested in history.

Nevertheless it is easier to enthuse the imagination with things that can be seen above street level where their vulnerability has civic impact.

Behind modern urban façades history crumbles into dereliction. The process is found in almost every town or village where irreplaceable walls and windows, plaster ceilings, fireplaces, halls and stairways, roofs and chimney stacks, exits and entrances are abandoned to decay. The precious domestic archeology of our forefathers awaits the demolition teams. It does not 'breathe or bleed' like the flora and fauna whose extinction we are arranging in our living, yet the loss to the quality of human life is almost as great.

Add archeology to your list of concerns. The task involved in finding out where threatened structures exist and applying for preservation orders, or securing listed building status, is not onerous. Conservation societies abound; enjoy the rewards of joining them. It will prove to be intellectually enriching.

INDEX

Access 70
Appeals 64-66, 67-68
Archeology 87
Aspect 70

Bureaucracy 11, 13, 18

Campaign:
  advice 41-51
  conduct 43
  initial moves 24
  introduction 12
  saving lost cause 68-69
  support gained 29-31
Car parking 28, 38
Civic beauty 8, 82, 87
Conservation 47
Cornwall 82-84
Countryside:
  blots on 70
  loss and destruction 1, 10, 82
  value of 22, 53-5

Death threat 30
Demonstrations   See Protest
Developers:
  aggressive and powerful 54-56
  lobby 35-36, 82-83
  reputations 26
  valley plans 26
Development:
  politics 13

points against 36-37, 38-40
points in favour of 24-25
presumption in favour of 58-59
rejection of 40
urban breathing spaces 78-79
valley site meeting 38-40
Department of Environment:
  appeals 64-66
  attitude to planning 58-59
District Councils:
  apparent peremptory behaviour 57
  appeals 65
  maladministration of 82-84
  meeting chairman of 34-35
  observer from 33-34
  observation of their meetings 35-36, 41, 51
  petitioning of 34, 51
  at site meeting 38-40
  timid 56
  villain of piece 54-56

Environment, Art for the 37
Environment, uniqueness of 18

Financial:
  consequences 29
  interests 10, 11, 22-23, 35-36
Fish farm development 73-75

Goodwill, loss of 75